Extraordinary Experiences: Tales of Special Needs Abroad

A *TALES FROM A SMALL PLANET* BOOK

Edited by Kathi Silva, Patricia Linderman,
Nicole Schaefer-McDaniel, Francesca Kelly and
Jennifer Dinoia

DEDICATION

Many thanks to the authors and editors who generously donated their time and energies to share these important stories.

This book is dedicated to people all over the world who are living with special needs and to those who help them experience the endless possibilities for adventure.

CONTENTS

A Note from The Editors   3

Foreword   7

Special Needs Abroad: A Framework   13

International Medicine Quest   21
By Bernadette Miller

My Daughter's Feet: Raising My Daughter With
Fibular Hemimelia in Zambia   29
By Kathryn Koonce

Snapshots into Life With Nagawa   37
By Kathleen Sheridan Mwanga

Moving Forward Despite Medical Trauma: 49
Imogen's Story
By Rachael Mackenzie-Meckel

No Peanuts Allowed: Living Overseas with Severe   59
Allergies
By Barbara Singer

Looking Forward: Discovering Europe with Lyme   69
Disease, My Wheelchair ... And Gusto
By Mary M. Al-Akhdar

Kolkata: The Veil of the Real   89
By L. York

Mindful in Madagascar   101
By Carolyn Parse and Jodi Harris

A "Stubborn Survivor" of Parkinson's Disease   113
By Paul Rohrlich

Getting Schooled in South Africa   121
By Sarah Showell

If in Doubt, Evacuate Right Away; And Don't Drink   133
the Water
By Lior Ben-Ami

Lessons in Silence: Disability, Not Inability   147
By Julia Inserro

My Daughter Through Joan of Arc's Eyes   153
By Suzanne Kamata

Ambassador for Autism   163
By Davie Silva

Wonder, Miracle, Gem...Merveille   171
By Cecile Dash

Remote Therapy Has Changed the Way We Think of   183
Face-To-Face Interactions
By Erin Long

An Atypical Childhood: Raising an Autistic Child in   191
Japan And Macau
By Kevin M. Maher

Let Me Hug Her: Elisa's Story   201
By Nayeli

Bridging a Cleft   211
By Elisabeth Weingraber-Pircher

Mari's Story: Can You Continue in the Foreign Service   221
After a Child's Life-Changing Diagnosis?
By Francesca Kelly and Mari O'Connor

Before Moving Overseas with a Special Need: A   237
Checklist

A Note from the Editors

This was not an easy book to write, and it has taken nearly three years to bring it to print. But we have made this a labor of love; one of our most touching projects to date. Whereas many people find it pleasant to talk about their adventures abroad, the exciting foods they eat, the amazing things they see and do, or the incredible people they meet, it took an extra bit of energy and courage to write about the journeys of adapting with a special need overseas.

Our authors are not professional writers but regular people who took the time, when often they had very little, to share their stories. They are proud of what they have done and how their overseas experiences have changed them. Finding an appropriate title for this book was also a challenge. While we feel the stories are inspirational and moving, we want to highlight the fact that they were written by ordinary people who, whether voluntarily or involuntarily, found themselves in extraordinary circumstances. These stories should be viewed neither as exceptional achievements nor any sort of "how-to" guide, but simply as a way of encouraging others to believe "If they can do it, so can I."

We have taken on an ambitious goal of sharing what it's like to have special needs as expats. It would be impossible to cover all types of special needs in all corners of the world, and everyone has a different story. Nor would we want to put everyone in the same category or suggest a one-size-fits-all model for overcoming obstacles. Obviously, a person with a physical disability will have different concerns from a person with a mental disability or a chronic illness.

However, there are common issues of concern that run through the book, including feeling comfortable about the quality of services in a foreign country, dealing with continuity of care when moving, facing feelings of how others view us (both as strangers in someone else's country and when the special need makes us stand out even more), finding support without family or long-standing friends nearby, and bridging language and cultural barriers that complicate communication with medical professionals.

Our goal was to share a variety of mostly positive experiences and advice from people who have triumphed in managing their challenges. Not every story has a tidy or happy ending, but the authors have learned how to come to terms with their situations and find personal growth in the process. By highlighting these personal struggles, what went well, and how we can make educated choices and guide our experiences in the right way, we hope we will encourage more people to step outside of their comfort zones, experience life abroad more fully, and open their hearts and minds to fellow human beings with special needs.

Terminology: "Special needs" is a broad term covering a wide range of diagnoses, and we have chosen to use this phrase for our book as our stories highlight people with mobility issues, cognitive disabilities, autism, birth defects, medical conditions, learning differences, chromosomal abnormalities, and mental illness. Our editors have taken great care to discuss terminology with our authors. For example, there are some who feel that a person is "autistic" and others who prefer the label of "someone with autism" — even within the autism community, this is a personal choice. Therefore, we left this and other sensitive terminologies up to the authors.

Foreword

My twins were born prematurely in the U.S., weighing less than one kilogram each, and strapped to all sorts of machines and wires for the first two months of their lives. Therapies began while they were still in the hospital with an occupational therapist "teaching" them how to swallow. The day we were able to bring them home, I remember the excitement of finally being able to dress them in the clothes we received from baby showers, even though the preemie onesies were still way too big on them, and it was a hassle to disconnect and reconnect the heart monitor machines they were required to use at all times. We had therapists coming to the house on a regular basis for that first eighteen months to teach the twins basic skills most babies learn on their own, such as how to sit, or how to stack blocks. But they were healthy, growing nicely, and making great progress, so we were cleared to go overseas with them and we were given a diplomatic assignment to Paris. We thought, "Wow, Paris! We're soooo lucky! What a dream!!"

We all believed it was a matter of time until the twins caught up to their peers and everything would be fine. But that's not how it turned out. After one year in France, I started to notice that the twins' language was regressing and they were becoming harder to interact with and discipline. Was it our move that had caused this? The bilingual French nursery they attended three mornings a week?

I loved being a new mother and loved our life in France, but Paris was not going well for our family. We flew back to the U.S. for testing and the twins were officially labelled with Pervasive Developmental Disorder Not Otherwise Specified (PDD-NOS), or on the autism spectrum. Early intervention with therapies was essential for a positive outcome. We assumed we could get the necessary therapies and treatments for them in Paris, a modern city with excellent medical facilities. To our surprise, we learned that the French are considered years behind the U.S. in autism interventions. We might as well have been in any developing country when it came to meeting our twins' autism needs.

We chose to cut our Paris assignment short and head back to the U.S. to set up an intensive therapy program. After two years of educating myself as much as possible about autism and providing my twins with what I hoped was the best barrage of therapies and support, we were ready to go overseas again. I am forever grateful for those years in my home country, where my children received care when they most needed it, and I could prepare myself with the wisdom and the tools I would need to be the most effective advocate and manager for their care abroad.

After Paris, we moved to four vastly different countries offering generally positive experiences, each one teaching me that local culture and institutions, as well as my research and involvement, have a lot to do with our twins' successful development.

Fast-forward 15 years to our diplomatic assignment in Uruguay, a tiny country in South America that is known for being slow-paced, a few years behind other countries, and challenging for foreigners. We assumed our twins would have a difficult time there, but we were pleasantly surprised to find that in Uruguay's harmonious culture and its emphasis on social relationships, our teenage twins were embraced, understood, and even admired. At that point in my twins' development, they didn't need structured speech and occupational therapy, but they did need positive interactions with people. For example, rather than working with a certified occupational therapist, we found Sebastian — an amazing Uruguayan personal trainer who had my twins running wacky obstacle courses, tossing weighted balls, and playing agility games on the beach. The twins loved these training sessions, and Sebastian became a mentor and a big part of why we loved Uruguay. I realized that just because a country doesn't have top-notch services, it doesn't mean it won't be a good fit for my children.

And from there, the idea for this book came about. I wondered if others had the same sense of curiosity as I did as to whether countries and cultures, regardless of how "developed" or not they are, can be receptive to expats with special needs. I hoped to find common denominators — clues — to help me determine if a country we were considering living in would not only provide the services my special-needs children required, but would have the right formula in other ways to make it a successful move for us. Would the culture be patient, tolerant, and kind to my quirky kids? Would I find the resources I needed to meet my children's physical, emotional, and social needs? Would the medical professionals have the same values and goals for my children as I do? Would the expat community surrounding me be supportive?

While working with the talented editors and inspiring authors for this book, I've found I'm not alone in wanting to share the news that the world provides us with more open doors than closed ones. There's no way to guarantee our overseas adventures will always be good, but there are specific things we can do and ways we can approach our experiences living or traveling overseas with special needs that will help. It's my sincere hope that every reader will gain something from these pages, whether it be the insight they're looking for, the sense that there is a tribe of like-minded people who believe a disability doesn't have to hold them back, or just some good, heartfelt stories from a distinctive population of expats.

Kathi Silva, October 2019

Special Needs Abroad: A Framework

While planning an international move for a person with special needs brings additional challenges, such as translating medical records, shipping medications across borders, or finding housing that allows for wheelchair mobility, there are many benefits to taking a cultural perspective on disabilities. Disability studies is a relatively new field, particularly when combined with cross-cultural issues, as these will govern general perceptions of people experiencing disabilities. Here are some questions that may be useful when deciding if, when, and where to make an international move:

How will the disability beliefs of the host culture affect our experiences?

The concept of disability differs among cultures. In fact, many languages don't have a single word for disability as English does. More commonly, people with specific types of impairments are grouped together and treated according to the social interpretation of that impairment. Is there a different perception for people with physical disabilities versus intellectual? Disabilities that began at birth versus others that developed later in life? Special needs that leave the person dependent on help versus someone who can live independently?

Even though modern science has shown that disabilities are caused by viruses, genetics, or accidents, cultures often still seek another reason for why a disability has occurred. This reasoning can affect how well individuals with disabilities are treated. In Southeast Asia, for example, the concept of karma is commo, where one's present life is determined by what one has done, right or wrong, in a previous existence. In some societies, people believe that children are born with a birth defect because the parents or their ancestors did something bad, and the disability is their punishment. A disability later in life may also be seen as a divine justice. Consequently, some individuals who are disabled can be ostracized and others fear that being closely associated with them will somehow indict them in the "crime." Our author Cecile Dash had first-hand experience with this, as she describes in her essay "Wonder, Miracle, Gem ... Merveille."

"In Congo, the stigma attached to having a handicap is harsh — people thought [she] was possessed by the devil and the family became outcasts."

Interestingly though, not all cultures find negative explanations. For example, Mexicans often believe that a certain number of disabled children are destined to be born, and that people who are especially kind and nurturing are "chosen" to be parents of these children (Madiros, 1989).

Our story from Nayeli, the mother of a Mexican child who was severely mentally and physically handicapped, shows this:

"... many people have told me, 'Let me hug her! Let me touch her!' and they feel that they are getting a positive vibration from my daughter. And yes, really, I think people like her were sent by God because He wants us to value our lives through them."

How will the cultural values of our host country affect our experiences?

Culture plays a big role in what a society values, and this can have an effect on the way special needs are perceived. It is not difficult to imagine that in less developed countries where mere survival is a priority, those with a disability will have a harder time accessing resources and support. And in societies where men appear to be valued more than women, there may be differences in perception between a disabled male and a disabled female.

Consider some societies, such as in Asia, where calling attention to oneself is improper and blending in with the larger community is a valued attribute. In these cases, anyone with a visible disability may feel particularly uneasy. We sense the discomfort of having an autistic child with abnormal behavior on Japanese public transportation in Kevin Maher's essay:

"The howling on trains, the inappropriate throwing of items ... all were becoming too much. The questions remained for most Japanese, 'Why would they allow him to do those things in public?'"

Cultures can be categorized as individual-based or collective-based. While individual-based cultures can be more likely to accept differences, when a society values collectivity, its members can be more likely to help one another, nurture the weaker members of that society, and have more patience and tolerance for those with greater needs. Davie Silva, a teen on the autism spectrum, contributed his thoughts about how people treat him abroad:

"This proves a point that to be around people like me you don't have to know too much about special needs, but you do have to treat special-needs people nicely. Even though the U.S. may have the most experience and knowledge about special needs, foreigners who are nice and patient and willing to try and understand me have sometimes been more helpful to me than the experts in the U.S."

What is the role of our doctors, therapists, and medical support team in our host country?

Culture can affect how we are expected to interact with medical professionals. In many societies that are structured hierarchically, doctors and medical workers are considered to be members of the upper socio-economical ranks and their word carries great weight. In this case, for example, any doctor asking the patients if a particular treatment seems acceptable would be highly unusual. Likewise, a doctor might find it offensive for a parent or patient to come prepared with questions about different treatment options or share their opinions about what the doctor is recommending. How will we cope if we are used to being a vital part of a treatment team, then become marginalized in our host culture? Or when the doctor in one culture is convinced of the "right" treatment, but doctors in the next culture have a completely different "right" treatment?

It is important that as expats, we are sensitive to this cultural nuance as it can create tension and stress between the relationship and may make visiting the doctor particularly unpleasant.

Themes about dealing with medical practitioners around the world are addressed in several of this book's essays. There is no doubt that this is a recurrent, core issue, even when the special need or disability is stable or has been resolved. In the essay "International Medicine Quest," the author talks of the various ways she receives medical care in each country:

"While I've now been managing my medical care overseas for over a decade, every move requires starting over. I still view this as a blessing — hey, you never know, maybe this doctor will have a hidden cure — but there is also a subtle fear that I could suffer a serious relapse in a location that is not well-equipped. Nonetheless, I remain optimistic that my breadth of experiences is beneficial overall."

While medical resources and technologies differ greatly throughout the world, it is not always the more developed, wealthier countries that provide the best quality care. Patients in Western countries often complain about feeling rushed in and out of appointments or being treated as a number or a case study. Medical malpractice suits mean doctors are more hesitant to think outside the box or suggest treatments that haven't been certifiably tested. Meanwhile, medical practitioners in some countries who do not have the luxury of using expensive machines and laboratories to diagnose or treat issues may have fine-tuned their intuition, and will spend more time listening to, touching and observing their patients. They may be more open to alternative treatments or more resourceful and open-minded about treatment plans. Kathryn Koonce touches on this in her essay about living in Zambia with a daughter born with fibular hemimelia:

"There is something about doctors in resource-limited settings. They need to rely on holistic approaches and intuition. They don't have fancy technology to diagnose. Because he is one of the only doctors who treats club foot in Zambia, he has seen a huge variety of cases."

How will my own culture and beliefs affect my transition?

In the United States, our system advocates independence, and our culture generally believes that self-sufficiency is a source of pride. When this self-sufficiency is disrupted, such as by moving to a country that is not handicapped-friendly, it could be very difficult to adjust this cultural value and accept help or come to terms with limitations without feeling stigmatized. If we come from a collective culture that emphasizes helping others, how difficult will it be to adjust to a country that is individual-based, where we expect more support from our community but don't get it? If we have been raised to divulge information comfortably and proudly about a disability to others, will we be able to function in a society that believes disability represents shame, guilt, or dishonor?

Cultural sensitivity requires being aware of the differences in values, beliefs and behaviors in other people. While we can't demand cultural sensitivity from others, we can incorporate it into our own values. If we are able to open our minds to what people in other cultures believe, or be flexible in what roles we and our medical teams play — even if it's different from what we think we want or need — it will help us adjust and react appropriately to the additional challenges of being in a foreign country with special needs. Author Elizabeth Weingraber-Pircher summarizes this beautifully:

"Science and medicine and their respective research do not follow universal standards and are key areas where culture becomes a main factor. It doesn't mean I should discard any advice from my doctors, nurses etc.; it means I have to consider their cultural norms and values as well as my family's cultural values and norms as equally legitimate and find a way that works for both, in the best interest of my family and my child, in the given context."

Every one of the essays in this book touches on this idea of cultural knowledge and flexibility. The authors, whether knowingly or not, have reflected on their values and what was important for them, and they have been able to let go or modify the less important aspects of their cultural comfort zone to adapt to life abroad. While it is no guarantee of success, adding a cultural perspective on disabilities can help soften some of the destabilizing realities of being far from home and provide unique opportunities for personal growth.

Reference

Kasomo, Daniel. Psychological Acceptance of Children with Developmental Disorders, Education 2012, 2(2): 11-15 DOI: 10.5923/j.edu.20120202.03

Madiros, M. (1989). Conception of childhood disability among Mexican-American parents. Medical Anthropology, 12, 55-68.

Stone, J. H. (2005). Culture and disability: Providing culturally competent services. Thousand Oaks: SAGE Publications.

International Medicine Quest

By Bernadette Miller

(Note: The author's name and a few details have been
altered to protect privacy.)

"Why you need so much medicine?" demanded the man
across the table from me. I sat inside a small, dimly lit room
just outside the airport cargo area. I felt like I was in an
interrogation room, as one man sat at the table and another
stood by the door, seemingly prepared to intercept any
attempt at escape. "Maybe you sell it? You drug dealer?"

I was surprised to find myself grateful to be wearing an
abaya, which aided my attempt at being a demure, passive
female, and I only wished that I had also covered my face to
hide the sudden tears welling up at the corners of my eyes.

"I have an illness," I said quietly. "I need this medicine. I
have to inject it every day. I would never sell it because I
need it. I wish I didn't have to take it at all." Why did I have
to justify this to strangers?

I hadn't wanted him to see my tears, but he could hear my
cracking voice. He seemed to soften.

"Here. Sign paper," he said, pushing a sheet printed in Arabic over to me. I signed it and stood up, walking away still slightly shaken.

The medicine arrived later, delivered to my home in Doha, Qatar. The stickers that said, "Keep Refrigerated" were strategically placed, as they always seemed to be, directly over the label text saying "Product of Israel."

————————

I had already lived in Doha, Qatar for several years when unsettling symptoms — loss of vision, the periodic inability to walk, a sudden loss of balance, amongst other problems — led me to seek medical care. The many doctors I saw in Qatar — all expatriates themselves, mostly from the Gulf region — struggled to diagnose me, so I ended up seeing a doctor in the U.S. She ran tests and quickly found a diagnosis: I had a chronic autoimmune disease.

As upset as I was to be facing a disease without a cure, I was relieved to have a diagnosis. I could start working on treatment and move ahead with my life. And I was determined that my life would continue to involve living and working overseas, which I loved.

Never mind that I needed daily injections of a highly specialized refrigerated medication manufactured in Israel, which was under a boycott by Qatar.

The Palestinian doctor in Doha who managed my care locally was familiar with the medicine. "Do not worry! I will treat you anyway," he assured me.

Getting the medicine through customs required me to visit the facility at the airport that my husband and I jokingly referred to as "the interrogation room." I wore an *abaya* — the long, black garment typically worn by women in the region, and gradually I felt more confident there, less prone to tears at the gruff inquiries of the customs agents. In fact, I started to see it as an adventure. How lucky and fortunate I was to be able to get the medication! And despite my initial discomfort at being alone with these men in a country where unrelated men and women can be punished for being together in physical proximity, I viewed it as a kind of forced cultural immersion. Sometimes, people seek out cooking, yoga, or language classes in a new country — in my case, I knew that my cultural adventures would involve finding ways to get my medication wherever we went.

I loved living in Qatar. My husband and I enjoyed our work and the way it opened up many career opportunities for us, and two of our three children were born there. The good life was made even easier with our superwoman housekeeper.

The medication worked well; my fear of injecting myself daily lessened, and I felt as if I could go about a normal life most of the time. However, due to my condition, I was even more severely affected than most people by the extreme heat in Doha, which could often reach 120 degrees Fahrenheit (almost 50 degrees Celsius) with high humidity.

I obtained a handicapped parking pass so I could use the spaces conveniently provided all over the city. Ironically, these were mainly empty, because disabled people in Qatar tended to stay home or live in institutions. If cars did park in the handicapped spaces, they were typically Land Rovers with dark-tinted windows and no permit.

One day, parking in a convenient handicapped space at the mall, I grabbed my two small kids and dashed through the suffocating heat to the entrance. A man shouted out to me in Arabic-accented English. "Yeah, lady, you look so handicapped." I badly wanted to return and explain, but between the heat and the sheer impropriety of a woman approaching a man, it was impossible. I didn't blame the Qatari culture for this. Invisible disabilities like mine are discounted everywhere.

After Qatar, I moved to Western Europe. There was a pharmacy on the same block as my apartment, and I could walk there in the blissfully cool weather. It took approximately three minutes to get there — maybe four if it was icy and slippery. The first time I showed up at the little shop with my prescription, the pharmacist apologized that she didn't have my medicine in stock, but assured me she would get it from another pharmacy later the same day. I almost laughed out loud. And when she called me two hours later to inform me that the medication had arrived, I almost cried with joy. The medicine quest in my new home was a short one!

I also loved my new neurologist in this country. She had a completely open attitude, willing to consider anything that would help me, with no bias toward any particular treatment. Instead, she focused on solid, current research, that she was always willing to explain to me in depth, and my own medical history. I still trusted and relied upon my doctor in the U.S., whom I continued to see occasionally. However, from my new perspective, I now recognized my American doctor's subtle push toward medications as a first-line solution. Surrounded by the dysfunctional U.S. medical system with its heavy influence from pharmaceutical companies, I suspect she wasn't even aware of this.

I found Western Europe to be an easy and enjoyable place to live. My husband and I loved it there, but it wasn't actually our dream. We really longed to live in isolated, exotic, intimidating places where others didn't want to go.

However, the matter of my medicine was always on my mind; I depended on it for my well-being, and I couldn't live in a place where I couldn't guarantee a supply of it.

With some short intervening assignments, and through a serendipitous and unexpected series of events, we eventually ended up in Bangkok. We found this an acceptable mix of the exotic and the convenient. I enjoy living downtown and experiencing the daily smells and sounds of the big city (although maybe not the traffic), but I still have easy access to grocery stores, medical facilities, and good schools. My medicine is not available locally, but I can bring in a one-year supply.

My physicians in Bangkok represent yet another doctoring philosophy. With refreshing humility, they admit that they know little about my condition, and they are happy to follow the recommendations communicated through me from my doctor in the U.S. Far from resenting this interference in their practice, they seem relieved to have guidance on how to handle my complicated case.

I have been able to manage my health care and my medicine and continue to live overseas with my family, as I had been determined to do. Yet I still struggle with one thing:

community. So far, I have resisted telling fellow expats about my condition. I want to be known for the person I am — enthusiastic and adventurous, and someone who loves immersing myself in new cultural challenges. Even with my employer, I hesitate to ask for special conditions or resources, putting more value on my privacy.

I'm afraid of wearing the label of my condition, concerned that it is the main thing people would see. I don't want to be pitied or treated differently. But that also means that I don't speak up on forums where I might meet other expats with experiences similar to mine. Surely we could benefit from sharing ideas, commiserating, and providing emotional support to each other.

I consciously give up that possibility, but I do find connection online. I'm a compulsive joiner of Facebook groups, and I've found some of the best support in groups where I don't even seem to belong at all. I love a group for Jewish expats, and I'm not Jewish. And "Flying While Fat," which I'm not particularly, has some of the best — and also most honest, sincere, and sympathetic — travel advice on the Internet, regardless of size.

While I've now been managing my medical care overseas for over a decade, every move requires starting over. I still view this as a blessing — hey, you never know, maybe this doctor will have a hidden cure (even now I'm experimenting with Chinese medicine in Asia) — but there is also a subtle fear that I could suffer a serious relapse in a location that is not as well-equipped. Nonetheless, I remain optimistic that my breadth of experiences is beneficial overall.

Like all expats, I have carved out a life full of compromises. I have created safe havens for my family in all of our homes, to balance out our wildly exhilarating adventures. We have had three children in international hospitals and experienced a variety of medical and educational philosophies around the globe. Looking back, I see that my experiences with doctors in the U.S., Europe, the Middle East and Asia gave me cultural insights I would not have gotten any other way. And my quest for medicine, from the intimidating "interrogation room" to a convenient European pharmacy in an Art Nouveau building, has just been part of the adventure. I wonder what the next country will bring.

This author, who chose to write under a pseudonym, has lived in four countries over the past six years. She is married to a U.S. Foreign Service Officer.

My Daughter's Feet: Raising My Daughter with Fibular Hemimelia in Zambia

By Kathryn Koonce

I have always had a thing about feet; I always notice them. I can remember the feet of many people who have entered my life. I still notice them — and even more now. In Zambia, I smile at the pudgy feet of babies and toddlers, and I notice the sometimes swollen and flexible feet of many women in Zambia.

I didn't know that feet would play such a prominent role later in my life. My beautiful daughter, born while we were on assignment in Zambia for our work in development, was born with a foot and leg deformity: fibular hemimelia (FH). FH is a blanket term for deficiency of the fibula, the bone that curves from the knee and meets the ankle bone. People with FH often have fewer than five toes. Naomi has four toes and a smaller foot on her FH leg. On top of this, she had a club foot: her foot was turned in when she was born.

I didn't know she had this abnormality while I was pregnant, but because her conception wasn't perfectly planned like her brother's, I had a nervous feeling. I had been in Zambia just weeks when I learned I was pregnant — a busy, stressful time. I was anxious and nervous about everything — deadly snakes, extraordinarily large and intimidating (yet mostly harmless) spiders, unfamiliar bacteria, illnesses. Of course, this was silly and small-minded. I was an anxious new mom in a new and unfamiliar place.

My pregnancy proceeded without any major events. After a short time, my fear of wild animals, insects, and bacteria waned as Zambia became more familiar to me.

Giving birth can be risky anywhere, but especially in Zambia, so we travelled to Massachusetts for Naomi's birth. The moment she was born I counted her fingers and toes as mothers instinctively do, and I noticed that her right foot was turned in and only had four toes. Her midwife and pediatrician told me she was perfectly healthy and not to worry about her foot. We would figure that out later.

She was immediately treated with the Ponseti method: a non-invasive way to treat her club foot by applying a plaster cast from her toes to knee, eventually stretching her flexible newborn foot into the correct position. She got a new cast each week on her right leg until she was about eight weeks old, and then she graduated to wearing braces on her feet with a bar between them to hold her feet in the correct place. This method helps the bones grow in the correct position.

We stayed in Massachusetts while Naomi continued her weekly casting and we got her passport in order. When she transitioned to the braces, they looked quite uncomfortable, especially as her feet were connected by a bar. In public, I noticed many children staring at her braces, wondering about them, and asking their parents. Ashamed parents hushed their children and told them not to stare. I only wished they had asked the questions they wanted to ask, so I began offering the information before any awkward hushing ensued.

With Naomi's new passport and braces on her feet, we were ready to return to Zambia. At this point we didn't know the extent of her fibular hememelia (a separate condition from club foot); we were in a "wait and see" period. With FH, the affected fibula grows more slowly than the other one, so the extent of the discrepancy becomes clearer as she grows.

I wasn't sure how Naomi's foot abnormality would be viewed in Zambia — a place where you almost never see anyone with physical deformities or disabilities, for a variety of reasons, including both the lack of good health care and stigmatization. My compassionate, stalwart nanny said: "For now, she's just a baby — just enjoy her." And we did.

Until she was six months old, Naomi wore braces all but one hour a day to keep her foot bones growing correctly. In Zambia and in Botswana, people were not shy about asking about Naomi's braces. I appreciated this. More than one person assumed that I put them on her so she wouldn't be able to crawl away. I proudly told people about the Ponseti method of correcting club feet — hoping that if anyone came across this common congenital abnormality, they would seek help, which is widely available through some humanitarian programs. I met a young man in Zambia who had received care from Naomi's great orthopedist who monitored her foot while we were in the country. He had a smile from ear to ear

— the surgery was life-changing.

Now, at the age of three and a half, Naomi only wears braces at night. Her FH leg is three centimeters shorter than the other, and that foot is about two sizes smaller than the other. She has lived all but a few months of her life in Zambia. Most days she doesn't wear shoes — when it's warm every day there is no need; children her age are almost always shoeless. She is not bothered at all by her "small foot" or "small leg." Most people do not notice; it's usually children who will look at her toes and count. I usually offer the information before they shy away from asking.

I had never heard of fibular hemimelia before Naomi was born with it. With my natural focus on feet, I have now noticed it much more. I've seen a few people in Lusaka with club feet, including adults with uncorrected club feet. I noticed a Zambian of Indian descent, probably in her late 30s, a few times in a local mall. After seeing her several times, I mustered up the courage to talk to her. I went to her and ventured, "I think you have what my daughter has?" I felt my face turn hot when she responded: "Your daughter had polio?"

I answered that no, she was born like this. The woman said, "She is lucky. You are American, yes? You have access to the best health care." We are indeed lucky. There are very few doctors who specialize in fibular hememelia. When Naomi was 15 months old, we learned that her FH needed to be treated before the age of two and a half. Her first cutting-edge treatment to straighten her tibia took place in Baltimore. The surgeon cut her bone and placed an Ilizarov frame (a metal frame with rods that go into the bone and pins holding it in place) on her lower leg to help the bone heal in the correct position (so it would no longer be curved). She had two metal rods in her tibia and four wires cutting through her flesh. This procedure looked like torture, but I did not take for granted the quality of the care she received and the fact that our health insurance paid for most of it.

In Lusaka, her Italian orthopedist proudly showed her X-rays to a Zambian doctor he was training. He noted that Naomi had received this treatment at the best place in the world for fibular hemimelia. He also noted she was getting world-class care for her club foot here in Zambia, and I agreed. There is something about doctors in resource-limited settings. They need to rely on holistic approaches and intuition. They don't have fancy technology to diagnose. Because he is one of the only doctors who treats club foot in Zambia, he has seen a huge variety of cases.

However, there are myriad challenges and limitations of health care in Zambia. My nanny, after visiting the orthopedist with us, asked, "Can doctors in Zambia do what Naomi had done to her leg?" I did not know how to respond. I didn't want to disparage this country that so warmly hosts my family. However, I have heard of too many avoidable deaths. There is only one doctor for every 12,000 people. I have visited crowded clinics where one doctor serves an enormous community. There are a few orthopedists, but most of them are foreign-trained and work at expensive private hospitals that are inaccessible to most people in Zambia.

I don't know how Zambians really feel about Naomi's foot. It's possible that some may think that I did something bad and this was God's punishment, or that someone was jealous of me and cast a spell on me. Witchcraft is still acknowledged in this proudly Christian nation. An acquaintance told me about her friend who had several miscarriages, but not to worry because she was now going to a traditional healer. She believed her friend was experiencing this misfortune because someone, jealous of her abundance of cows, had placed a curse on her. There is a Witchcraft Act penalizing individuals who practice witchcraft used to cause harm to others. Serious stories about witchcraft pepper the main national newspapers.

These facts and stories stick in my mind along with my work on gender inequality. I have read too many news articles about girls as young as two being "defiled." A Zambian friend who runs a popular health-related blog told me that some witch doctors advise men to steal their "star" or their innocence to gain wealth or success. Based on these stories, I am careful about the men I allow in Naomi's life. At a weekend getaway, a child-minder was offered to us, to stand outside our chalet so my husband and I could get away for dinner. Expecting a woman and instead seeing a man, my stomach knotted and I immediately said no — I will not leave my sleeping daughter and son in the care of a man I do not know.

Despite my occasional fears, overwhelmingly I appreciate Zambians' unabashed curiosity about Naomi's foot. I love how Zambians view children as truly joyful. I was surprised to hear a young man say, "I can't wait to have children; they bring so much joy." I will not forget Naomi's dancing to the music made by our close-knit group of Zambian nannies, with their beautiful voices and makeshift drums.

Naomi has no major limitations, though she probably will not be a ballerina (due to the lack of range of motion of her ankle). She currently has a three-centimeter length discrepancy and wears a lift in her shoe. Naomi matter-of-factly notes that she has a big foot and a small foot and a "special leg." I hope it stays this way, but I know it will not. We move to another country every four years. I do not know where we will be when she is a teenager and will start to care about how her body looks. Maybe we can use a cultural difference to our advantage. In the U.S. she could cover her leg with tattoos (and I would be ok with that). In the Middle East or in some parts of Africa it would be appropriate for her to cover her legs anyway. Maybe there is a culture we have yet to discover where the people consider limb differences to be sacred.

As an American child living abroad, Naomi will be different wherever she is. I hope she will carry her determination and strong will with her as she braves another harrowing procedure to lengthen her FH leg. Though this is not easy, we are lucky to have access to procedures that will get both of her feet touching the ground. In the meantime, I hope her continued experiences will keep her head in the clouds or her imaginary world with her best friend Masha Shasha, a Russian-speaking fairy with a small foot and small leg who follows us wherever we go. I am sure that living among other cultures will only enhance her uniqueness and help her continue to be resilient and embrace her differences.

Kathryn Koonce grew up in Newtown, Connecticut. After serving in Russia with the Peace Corps, she moved to New York City, where she found her niche in international development and met her husband. Kathryn and her husband moved to Zambia on their son's first birthday; their daughter was born less than a year later. Kathryn and her family now live in fairy-tale-beautiful Kyiv, Ukraine.

Snapshots into Life with Nagawa

By Kathleen Sheridan Mwanga

Patongo Internal Displaced Persons (IDP) Camp, Northern Uganda, Jan. 2008

Standing at the table, drinking my last sips of coffee and brushing aside the breadcrumbs left on the wooden slats, I pick up the newspaper — a rare sight in this IDP camp, where I was working for a humanitarian aid organization. Someone must have driven through a faraway town yesterday, I think to myself. I'm drawn by my curiosity to see what the current news may be, feeling a bit oblivious to it all in the dust and heat of northern Uganda. Flipping through the pages quickly, eager to get on my bike for the seven-minute ride to work, my eye catches an image of a girl who obviously has Down syndrome. Her features, instantly familiar to me because of my own sister with Down syndrome, are only a physical sign to me of the beauty and talent that these people have.

I read the headline, "Victim of Genetic Disorder," and a lump develops in my throat. My heart sinks, and I continue reading the description of a girl who is simply described as "stupid" by the people in her slum neighborhood. The negative connotation toward this disability is clearly conveyed in the story, with an unmistakable tone of pity, sorrow and despair. At the end of the article, the phone number of a neighbor was included, as well as the name of the mother, Melida, who fried cassava for a living. Melida had only recently been told of the Down syndrome diagnosis of her 8-year-old daughter, Nagawa.

On my next visit to Kampala, during a weeklong R&R trip, I traveled to the slum with the newspaper in my hand, together with a Ugandan man, Kafero, whom I was just starting to date. I knew right then that Kafero was a special man when he embarked on this adventure with me; little did we know that it was the start of a lifelong commitment together. We wandered for hours, hoping to meet the mother and daughter. We were directed from one mud house to another, and finally to a particular tin-roofed structure that was quite dark to enter. There, we were able to talk with some elders wearing long white *kanzu* (traditional Ugandan wear for men). The floor was dirt, and some sunlight streaming in through a makeshift window illuminated the goat meat and sauce they were enjoying together.

The men proceeded to bring us to a home of a mother and daughter with cerebral palsy. We greeted them, spoke briefly and continued searching for Nagawa and her mother. We finally found the office of the mainstream newspaper that had printed the article. Fortunately, the young woman who had written the article was in the office, and she guided us through the maze of dirt paths, over the open gutters and sewers, and eventually to the girl's home. Nagawa, missing some teeth and dressed in an old Barney nightgown, came bounding out of her home, thrilled to see some visitors. Her mother Melida was there, smiling and seeming slightly confused. As we sat down to talk with her, Kafero did all the translating, showing her pictures of my sister and previous students I had worked with in the U.S. with Down syndrome, and explaining all they were able to do and could potentially do. Melida seemed to recognize this and was hopeful and encouraged. Limited by her lack of knowledge of the disability and its manifestations, she was confused as to why Nagawa could only grunt and not speak, although she did understand the local language, Luganda. As we began a friendship with Nagawa and her mother, we emphasized the importance of education and opportunity for Nagawa.

Over time, we became regulars in the neighborhood and frequently visited Nagawa and Melida. As we shared books and encouraged Melida to enroll Nagawa in school, her eyes began to open up to Nagawa's potential. With some convincing of the headmaster of a local school in the area, he accepted her into a class. We supported her in obtaining a uniform, school shoes, socks and a school bag.

With Melida, we maintained a close relationship and strongly believed it was most beneficial to support her in starting a small business which would enable her to make more income to support herself and her three children. We spent some time asking Melida to do some research as to what sort of small business she could maintain and manage in her neighborhood, and she decided that having several large bags of charcoal, stored in a shed, would allow her to sell it in small amounts and make a profit. She would then sell small pieces to local people in her neighborhood. This seemed to give her a sense of ownership over the betterment of her family.

We visited often, and after winding through the twisting paths between houses and ravines, turned the final corner to the humble tin-walled house where they lived. There was a tall tree protruding from the top of that small area that made it easier to locate. Melida could usually be found doing household chores, with Nagawa eagerly helping to wash dishes in a small plastic basin. Their interactions were loving and patient, and Melida understood Nagawa's sounds very well, even if they were unintelligible to others. If they weren't at home when we arrived, they could be found on the empty veranda in another area of the neighborhood where Melida sold her fried cassava, and Nagawa would be helping usher customers in. Melida's charcoal business was also thriving.

Occasionally we took Nagawa out on visits around Kampala, such as to church and out for chicken and chips, which was her favorite treat. We also joined her on a school trip to Lake Victoria and a visit to the airport. One particular day, the three of us took local transportation to Entebbe Zoo together, and Nagawa was amazed at the animals' size, their closeness and their sounds. Her mom was happy to have her go out and explore the city for the day with us, and she listened intently to Nagawa's stories, mostly expressed through her hands and sounds. Melida clearly loved her dearly, and their relationship was beautiful and strong.

London, England, November 2009

Chopping vegetables and preparing for Thanksgiving, our second in England, Kafero and I crossed off the dishes we had made and decided to take a break from those we were still preparing. We loaded some money on Skype and called Nagawa's headmaster, who had a phone, and reached out to him to see how everyone was. I was accustomed to calling on holidays and checking in on those we cared about. It was then that we heard the news — Melida had recently died. As Nagawa had left for school one morning, her mom was showering at their home and had a heart attack and died instantly. Since her father had passed when she was just a toddler, she was now left without living parents, in a slum, as a young girl with a disability and without communication skills.

We remained in England for a few months after that, but we returned to Uganda in January 2010 and met the auntie with whom Nagawa and her brothers were living in the same neighborhood. We built a relationship with the auntie and continued regular visits with Nagawa while we explored employment options back in Uganda. Nagawa was still her vibrant self, but she had clearly endured a tremendous loss with her mother dying so suddenly. It was on her mind a lot, as she would repeatedly go through the detailed story of bringing her mom to the village many hours away to bury her. Although her words were still limited, she communicated the story both with her hands and her eyes.

Kampala, Uganda, August 2010

Married just two weeks, and permanently moving back to Kampala to teach, we met with Nagawa's aunt and spoke about the vulnerability of Nagawa in the neighborhood. The auntie told us of her limited capacity to care for her own five children, plus the additional three of her brother's children. We agreed to have Nagawa join our family and move to the other side of the city.

Nagawa joined the kindergarten class at the International School of Uganda, which was a few years below her expected age level, but developmentally appropriate. Unfamiliar with the expat community and school, it took time for her to adjust. However, making friends came easily, as socializing was her favorite thing to do. Despite being so limited in her expressive language, she didn't hesitate to walk up to someone and greet them, smiling, and joking around. She could read people's emotions quite well, and if she didn't feel welcome, she would move on.

Nagawa has quite a strong level of energy, so this can be intimidating for some people at first; however, most Ugandans are very accepting and welcoming to her. In fact, they tend to be very curious, which can lead to many stares, but people are kind to her, asking questions to understand more. We always took these as positive signs, because people are trying to understand something new or unexpected to them, and the more they know, the more compassionate and accepting they can be.

With speech therapy at a clinic at the government hospital, her grunts turned into intelligible speech, and words began to form. It took four months to teach her to say her name "Na-ga-wa," modeling the sounds, segmenting, and using a mirror. The longer someone was around her, the more obvious it was just how bright she was, despite her limited verbal skills. The small suburb of Kampala where we lived included both high-walled compounds with armed guards and settlements with tin-roofed mud houses, but Nagawa balanced between the two: living, schooling and socializing amongst the upper-class Ugandans and expats, while also being drawn towards the local children of the neighborhood. Stared at and questioned initially, she soon became well-known and popular amongst the neighborhood children.

There was a group of about ten to 15 local kids who lived behind our school gate in a little shanty-type makeshift housing settlement, which most of the expats would just drive by. However, for Nagawa, this was her comfort zone. She was drawn to the women cooking outdoors with charcoal and the kids running around outside and playing with locally handcrafted toys. Nagawa would invite them up to our house, and they would walk up the hilly road, several with babies tied on their backs. They usually played outside in the yard with balls, dolls and puzzles. My husband, Kafero, would help make local porridge for them, and they would line up on the ledge of the veranda and enjoy the sweet treat.

On other occasions, Nagawa would be invited to birthday parties for classmates, which would often be at a gated diplomat's house in an expensive neighborhood in Kampala. There would be a clown to entertain the children, hors d'oeuvres around the pool, kiddie cocktails, a bouncy castle and face painting. Nagawa became a bridge between the local and foreign communities within the neighborhood, crossing back and forth frequently and rather effortlessly.

The legal and final adoption of Nagawa was finalized in early 2011, and she became a permanent member of our family. Maintaining a relationship with her auntie and brothers has been crucial, and visits back to her old neighborhood prove to some that she is a walking miracle. The girl once called degrading names can now speak, understand and communicate, express herself and have a voice. There would sometimes be stares of disbelief, with people whispering and stopping in their tracks to ask if that is indeed "Nagawa?!"

January 2018

Nagawa attended the international school until Grade 8, when she was 15, and she has since attended various vocational programs within Uganda that integrate functional skills and independent living abilities for her future. Through this, she has learned ceramics, beadwork, creating handmade cards, candle-making and general skills to take care of herself. She's done internships in our school kitchen and at a local school for young children with disabilities. She loves her church community, her friends, attending youth group and doing independent tasks around our neighborhood. She has her own mobile phone now and can call a friend to ask if she wants to come over, or call a neighbor for a ride to church.

As I walk around our neighborhood, at the local grocery store and on the streets, people all seem to know Nagawa. I'm forever called "Mama Nagawa," and she's popular among all local employees, *boda* (motorcycle) drivers and children. Every single employee in the grocery store greets her by name, inquiring about how she is doing and what she is learning at school. They smile as she completes the shopping, often on her own, and they laugh as she banters back and forth with them. She has a confidence about her that she carries proudly, one where she can "hold her own" with people now, which I attribute to her newfound ability to communicate. She occasionally will walk past the greeter at the supermarket, responding that she is "too busy shopping" to greet them, then turn around, giggle and wave cheekily. The guards greet her as she enters any premise around our neighborhood, and the *boda* drivers even ask me how she's doing if I'm alone.

I am not sure if being adopted by an expat might have shifted some locals' view of her as a person with a disability. I say this because, culturally, people with disabilities here are often unknown, hidden, and can be seen as "unwanted." Witnessing someone from abroad who has indeed very much "wanted" a child like her may have changed their perception of the value of such individuals. Nagawa herself has undeniably changed the views of people with disabilities within the local population of Ugandans in our community. I can now only hope that their view can be brought back to their homes and villages, because they now see what is possible when someone like Nagawa is given a chance, and given the dignity to live a full life.

Having Nagawa as part of our family has also opened up doors to support other local families with children who have Down syndrome. As we travel frequently out and about in villages, the community and the city, I actually quite often see a child with Down syndrome, and I always take the opportunity to talk with the parents. I'm naturally drawn to these individuals, no matter what country I am in, because of the positive experience growing up with my sister. Here in Uganda, I especially love connecting Nagawa with other children with Down syndrome, so take the opportunity whenever it presents itself. I sometimes have to navigate the conversation carefully to determine if they are aware of their child's needs and diagnosis, as sometimes they are not. If Nagawa is with me, they are pleasantly surprised at the common connection we have and very curious as to what she is able to do at this stage in life. I usually take the chance to share a few photos of my sister, and they sometimes are surprised to learn about a person in another country with the same condition as their child. It's standard to gather their contact information to be able to stay in touch, and they are always very curious to see Nagawa, as she is now a young adult who can help them envision their child's future progress.

We have had several gatherings and picnics with these families, with the mom, dad, siblings, and some grandparents and aunts and uncles coming together. It's been such a positive experience for all involved, because everyone thrives on community, and especially those whom we can relate to, even across cultures. It's also an opportunity for resource sharing, with discussions on school options, doctors, speech therapists and community connections around Kampala.

By sharing personal success stories of Nagawa and also my sister's journey through life, we can offer testimony of what is possible for these remarkable individuals. It's been a true joy to be able to build a network of support and connections for these families, and many have expressed how they feel solidarity with the others and added strength in knowing that they are not alone in navigating this journey.

An article in a newspaper and a chance meeting, now over ten years ago, developed into a beautiful relationship, with our family eventually fusing together. I'm so thankful for Nagawa as an individual and what she has done by being her confident and bold self in Uganda. Nagawa has been a catalyst for relationships that wouldn't have been possible without her. Person by person, she continues to change the perspectives of those she encounters.

Originally from the wildwoods of Michigan's Upper Peninsula, Kathleen Sheridan Mwanga began globe-trekking at the age of 19. Teaching in the Pacific Northwest and spending a summer with the Tibetans in the Himalayas of northern India inspired her to work with people at a disadvantage due to war and conflict. Sadly, in 2014 her husband was diagnosed with a rare form of cancer, and he passed away in November 2015. She now lives in Addis Ababa, Ethiopia, with her four children and works as a special education teacher at an international school. The family enjoys safaris and spending time outdoors, as well as music, poetry and arts events. She reports that through all this, they have learned that "taking risks to explore new places always leads to new moments and memories, supporting the arts in our community is a priority, and our moments on earth here together are for loving."

Moving Forward Despite Medical Trauma: Imogen's Story

By Rachael Mackenzie-Meckel

As an Australian, all I ever wanted to do was travel to see other countries. It's almost in our blood that as soon as an Australian finishes university, he or she immediately looks for work overseas. I was given the chance to relocate to Amsterdam at the age of 28 and grabbed the opportunity with both hands, having no idea what the future would hold or where my life would take me.

As the stars would have it, I met my American husband while working in the Netherlands, and we agreed that what we wanted most out of our marriage was adventure and experiences, never to be burdened by the drudgery of day-to-day life. How young and naive we were!

My husband works in the oil industry, and as many fellow expats know, that generally means moving countries every three to four years. We have been lucky enough to enjoy expat stints in Europe, America, Australia, Asia and now South America.

Amid these global adventures, we managed to create three beautiful children, an eldest boy followed soon after by a twin boy and girl. We were thrilled to show our children the gorgeous beaches of Australia and the snow-capped mountains of Colorado and have them walk hand in hand with orangutans in Indonesia.

However, our wish of never wanting a "normal" life was starting to show its true colours. The first king hit to our family came when our beautiful daughter, Imogen, one of the twins, was diagnosed with a rare form of leukaemia while we were living in Perth, Australia. We were back in Australia because my husband had been transferred there for his work. We reeled with disbelief: our tiny, seemingly healthy 8-month-old daughter was to start chemotherapy a day after she was diagnosed. How was this possible? Without family nearby for support (my immediate family lived in New South Wales, a five-hour plane trip away) and two other children to care for, we were at our wits' end trying to deal with the situation.

Meanwhile, our daughter was confined to the paediatric oncology ward in Princess Margaret's Children's Hospital in Perth. We spent virtually all of our days at the hospital for the next six months, trying to juggle the other children and my husband's work while caring for our daughter at this critical time. An adventure? No, it was a nightmare.

Incredibly, my husband's employers gave him every Wednesday off to visit Imogen at the hospital, so that helped share some of the burden. As Imogen made steps forward with her treatment, we were also blessed to have the support of our friends in Australia. They cooked baby food for our other twin, helped with household chores, took our other kids for playdates and called regularly to see what they could do to help. My family came over as often as they could, and my husband's family came out from America to stay for a few weeks, and we were forever grateful for their love.

To cut a long story short, Imogen made an amazing recovery from her disease, and she was allowed to come home at 18 months of age. At first, we presumed we would never get back on the expat bandwagon again, but after careful thought and discussions with her doctors, we decided that if Imogen was well, we would get back out there and start living our lives again and offer our children the rare experiences we knew we couldn't get just staying put.

And so we were off again! First Houston for a few years, and then on to Jakarta, which would prove to be our most exotic posting and also the most difficult. Jakarta, with its chaotic lifestyle and charming locals, tested us as we had never been tested before. Our eyes, ears and noses experienced sights, sounds and smells we had never encountered. It was wild and slightly dangerous and exotic all at once, but the kids just slid right in, much to our amazement. They were becoming the global citizens we wanted them to be.

However, any expat who has had a child with health issues would likely agree that the hardest part about a new country is finding the right medical people to deal with your particular issues. In our case, we had to find an oncologist we felt comfortable with as well as a good paediatric cardiologist, as Imogen had ongoing heart issues due to the intensity of her chemotherapy treatment at such a young age. Jakarta is NOT well known for its top-notch health care professionals. Specialists were difficult to find, and we were not overwhelmed by the credentials of many of them.

Finally, we decided that travelling to Singapore every few months to see specialists was the best answer. This was an expensive option, as we were not covered by insurance for Imogen's heart issues (considered to be a pre-existing condition), but we could not put a price on her wellbeing. Our international health care policy covered most of our requirements, but if you have experienced any medical issues in the past, insurance providers can be very tough on what they choose to honour.

And then our story took another devastating turn. We were living in a magnificent house in the expat suburb of Kemang in Jakarta. Despite the stifling humidity, occasional rats, insane traffic jams and the general assault on our nostrils of decaying garbage on the streets, we were very happy.

However, this was all about to change. One particularly humid Monday morning at 6 a.m., the kids were getting ready for school as they did every weekday morning. We were all running about gathering lunch boxes and loose shoes and uniforms, and I was preparing their breakfast. The boys were tucking into their cereal when Imogen's twin brother, Nick (who was now eight) noted that Imogen wasn't downstairs; he could hear her crying upstairs. He said to me, "That's not a normal cry, Mum." Dropping what I was doing, I made my way up the stairs, thinking she must have fallen over or couldn't find her skirt — something simple surely.

But it wasn't something simple. As I approached the top of the stairs, I saw that Imogen was leaning on a wall between her bedroom and the bathroom. She was crying and leaning awkwardly and had wet herself — a very unusual occurrence for her. I walked toward her, talking soothingly and explaining it was OK and we'd just pop her in the shower and clean her off. What I didn't notice at the time is that her right arm was hanging limply, and she was slurring her words slightly. I thought it was because she'd just woken up.

My husband was showering at the time, so I led Imogen into the bathroom, and it was at that exact moment that I noticed what was really happening. Her mouth had dropped on the right-hand side. I felt like my heart had stopped. Imogen was having a stroke at the age of eight. I screamed at my husband to wrap her in a towel and put some clothes on her. He was shaking and we were both in shock, unable to believe what was happening.

Luckily, we had a driver on hand and as it was early in the morning, the heaving Jakarta traffic hadn't reached its peak yet. My husband stayed at home with the boys while I cradled Imogen in my arms and we made our way to the local expat clinic, which was in no way equipped to deal with an emergency such as this. On the way I rang my neighbour and best girlfriend, who was also Australian, to explain what had happened. She almost dropped the phone in shock and was immediately at our house for support. I don't know what we would have done without our friends during this time. We had support from a lot of the mothers in the school who were from many different nations including Indonesia, as well as the friends we spent a lot of time with in our neighbourhood who included Australians and British couples.

The expat medical centre was woefully inadequate; I almost felt I had to diagnose Imogen myself. There was one expat doctor there, but the local nurses and staff were virtually useless. They just put her on a drip and said she needed to be monitored. They didn't have an MRI to see what was actually happening to her brain, and they explained that we needed to go to another medical facility, but that would take at least an hour in peak traffic. Imogen was stable at this stage, but the stroke was now visible: she could not speak properly and her right arm and leg were semi-paralysed. Her mouth drooped significantly. We were devastated and in shock and all we wanted to do was get out of there, but to where?

In the meantime, our friends had arrived at the hospital, bringing food and offering words of support for us all. My husband was frantically trying to arrange a medical flight to Singapore that our insurance would pay for but, incredibly, there were no private planes available to take us there. Finally, with no progress being made on transport, we contacted the local airlines and were able to get a flight out to Singapore, but we still had the nightmare of driving her to the airport which could take up to three hours in Jakarta traffic. Finally, we managed to get into a beaten-up ambulance with an ancient oxygen tank by her side and a nurse who looked like she'd graduated a week ago as our chaperone.

Eighteen hours after Imogen had her stroke, we landed in Singapore and were rushed to Mount Elizabeth where she finally received her MRI that confirmed she had suffered an ischemic stroke to the left side of her brain, damaging the part responsible for coordination.

While we were obviously grateful to be in a country with the doctors and medical equipment that Imogen required, the next few weeks were very difficult for all of us. Once again, Imogen amazed us with her fighting spirit. The day after the stroke she was introduced to the top neurologists, cardiologists, physiotherapists, and occupational therapists who worked on her recovery daily. I was heartened that she responded so positively to her caregivers, working very hard to do the exercises she was given and not complaining once about the invasive MRI or echocardiograms. She kept a smile on her face, even while her mouth was still a little crooked!

We loved the fact she had a clean private room and one-on-one attention from the kind nurses. The neurologist was even open-minded enough to suggest we see an acupuncturist, who used his needles to try and gain more mobility in Imogen's hand and foot.

Two weeks later, Imogen was again able to speak properly; her mouth righted itself and she was happy and smiling, chatting with all the medical staff and eating well. We were delighted at her recovery, but sad to think that our little girl who had already been dealt a tough life was experiencing yet another setback.

One might think that this latest medical drama would force our family to finally stop and go back home, whether it be the U.S. or Australia. However, having been away from our countries for ten years, we just couldn't pack up and go home, wherever that was, and there was my husband's job to consider. So, we decided to return back to Jakarta, and a year later we moved to Kuala Lumpur in Malaysia, where we found some great specialists to help Imogen as she continued to improve in leaps and bounds.

Two and a half years later, we now find ourselves living in Montevideo, Uruguay, where my husband's work has taken us. Once again, we had to look for those same specialists to help monitor Imogen's progress, but we don't take things as lightly anymore. This time we know where we can go immediately to get help, and we have made sure our medical insurers know our situation and how they can best assist in case of emergency.

However, it's still a struggle to find the right medicines she requires daily, as her drugs have different names in different countries, and the doses can differ also. Language barriers are very difficult, especially when trying to explain medical terms, and her medical records are so skewed, as I've had to gather them from five different countries often in different languages. At one stage I wrote down everything that happened to her and filed it on paper and transferred to disc, so I could use it every time we moved again. It's not easy.

It's been five years since Imogen's stroke, and every day we touch wood that she will be able to keep moving forward and not face as many dramas as she had in the past. We're not naïve anymore and realise that wishing for adventure also means having the ability and strength to cope with the unforeseen misadventures.

Imogen attends school along with her brothers and has many friends wherever she goes. She still has a slight disability with her right hand and foot, but mentally, she's alert and very intelligent. Prior to the stroke, she wrote with her right hand. Now she's taught herself to write with her left. We have hired an occupational therapist and physiotherapist to work with her weekly, and she continues to make progress.

Will she ever have full mobility again? Probably not, but she is living her life to the fullest, and her experiences have made her wise beyond her years. Imogen has the innate ability to put her friends at ease no matter what problem they're experiencing at school. She takes the lead in most class discussions and does so methodically and with reason, always willing to listen to others' viewpoints. Despite the fact she no longer does a lot of sports due to her weakened heart, she has never been bullied because she's so matter-of-fact about what happened to her, and this puts the other children at ease. They accept her limitations as she does and never make an issue out of it.

We never felt that we failed our daughter by moving countries, and despite the challenges she has faced, we believe she is a better person for having been able to deal with her problems in an international environment. Imogen and her brothers are truly global citizens — when we hear them speak in different languages and see the empathy they have for those from different cultures, we know we did what was right for our family. Imogen knows that she is capable of handling anything, and that's more than we could have hoped for.

Rachael Mackenzie-Meckel is an Australian married to an American geologist and has been living around the world with her family for the past 20 years. She is a former radio journalist and communications writer who enjoys travelling, spending time with family and friends, and exploring new countries. She also writes a blog on her other passion, interior design, called www.nomadbydesign.net that features expat houses and gives tips on how to make a house feel more home-like, no matter where you live in the world. She is a proud mother to Imogen and her twin brother Nicholas and older brother Jasper.

No Peanuts Allowed: Living Overseas with Severe Allergies

By Barbara Singer

When you move to a foreign country, one of the first things you do is learn customary greetings and pleases and thank yous in the local language to help you settle into your new surroundings. Our family also learns how to say the word "peanut" in the local language. It might seem like a strange word to want to know immediately, but to us it is among the most important pieces of our foreign language vocabulary. To prioritize this word gives us some peace of mind overseas.

We were living in our home country of the United States when we learned that our 18-month-old daughter, Alex, was allergic to peanuts. I was eating a peanut butter and jelly sandwich, and Alex, as many toddlers do, decided whatever was in my hands must be something that she needs. So, she grabbed for my sandwich and took a bite.

I remember a flash of thought at that moment — should I let her have the sandwich? I am a maternal/child health specialist, and my husband is a physician. We both keep an eye on the science related to peanut allergies and their relationship with pregnancy, childbirth, and breastfeeding. I knew that there had been back-and-forth recommendations over the years about when you could introduce peanuts to young children. Because the science was so unclear, my response was probably too relaxed about letting her touch the sandwich.

She took one bite of the peanut butter sandwich and immediately started crying. Her baby face turned red, hives emerged all over her little body and her eyes began to swell shut. She was panicking; her father and I were panicking, but we were able to medicate her with some over-the-counter antihistamines to slow the reaction and then took her to the emergency room. A doctor's appointment a few days later confirmed what we had already figured out: Alex was allergic to peanuts.

After her diagnosis, what we initially perceived as a minor inconvenience would fundamentally alter the way we lived our lives. This became abundantly clear on the day we received a call that no parent wants to get: the call from day care saying your child is having trouble breathing.

Luckily, the day we received that call my husband was just around the corner at home. He instructed the day care to hang up and call 911 immediately. He was able to get to the day care within five minutes and could see Alex struggling to breathe, so he quickly administered an EpiPen. The ambulance arrived, and he went with our daughter to the hospital, where the doctors kept her under observation for ten hours. This is standard, since the symptoms of the allergy can return when the effect of the EpiPen wears off, and more epinephrine may need to be administered. Eventually she was declared "fine" and was discharged.

Except it wasn't all "fine" for us; in fact, it was quite a scare and a glimpse into what could happen if we, or anyone we entrust with our daughter's care, were not diligent with her newfound allergy. We later learned what happened — the school had forgotten to tell a new family that peanuts were not allowed and that family sent a peanut butter sandwich in their child's lunch. Alex, just 3 years old, inhaled the smell of peanut butter and started to feel itchy. Then she broke out into hives and began coughing and crying. Her day care providers weren't sure what to do and called us. We found out the care providers, all from Central and South America, did not know much about peanut butter as it was something they hadn't grown up with, and so couldn't pick it out amongst all the sandwiches. They just didn't recognize the smell.

It took that scare to help us truly understand the power of allergies and that we could not let our guard down. We had been lucky this time but may not be the next, as we learned that every reaction can be different. After that incident, we were clear with our instructions to everyone caring for Alex, "Call 911 first, us second." This was good advice until we decided to take the plunge and move overseas to a country with no 911 system, and a subpar medical system in general.

My husband worked in global health, and I aspired to be a professional traveler. The timing of the job offer overseas was good, and we were ready to move abroad. I was just finishing up my Ph.D. and I would soon need to move on to my next gig, whatever that would be. Alex was not yet in primary school, so there was little disruption to consider. As we went through the long process to facilitate our first overseas post, we thought the peanut allergy might be an issue for obtaining the State Department's medical clearance. But in the end, Alex was cleared, so off we went to Malawi, aptly known as the "warm heart of Africa."

This was our first time stepping foot in Africa, let alone living there, so we were not sure what to expect. We understood before going that Malawians consider peanuts (referred to as groundnuts) a staple food, but we did not anticipate that they would be cultivated in just about any available piece of land! In hindsight, we were so excited to go overseas that we failed to do more research in advance, such as reaching out to the post health unit, school or social sponsor with allergy questions.

Looking forward, as more experienced parents and expats, we are now more inquisitive so we can be better prepared for what to expect. Generally, we see living and traveling overseas as manageable with my daughter's allergy, although there are a few posts that we would really have to think hard about, given how prolific peanuts are in the cuisine and environment.

What we did know prior to moving to sub-Saharan Africa was that allergies were not common and therefore not well understood. However, we were surprised to learn that no students in our chosen school — expats or locals — had any nut allergies. We realized the onus was on us to educate the school on this issue.

From the start, the school administration asked us to assist them in developing an approach that would keep Alex safe. We were relieved that they took the allergy very seriously, but I understood why. After all, we were living in a country where access to emergency medical care was essentially non-existent. When Alex walked in on that first day mid-year, the school had issued a new "no peanut" policy in the primary school and posted signs on every classroom door stating NO PEANUTS ALLOWED. My gut instinct at the time was that this was a bit of an overkill approach. However, since that time we have been enrolled in other post schools where the pendulum swung the other way, meaning there was little interest in regulating peanuts at the school, and as a result, we have had several more reactions. So given the two choices, I prefer an approach that is more cautious.

However, that choice comes with consequences. On that first day, instead of just being a "new student," Alex was known as the "peanut allergy kid." Even as we met new families at post, they referred to us as the family with a peanut allergy. It is hard enough for our kids to pick up and move to a new country, new home and new school, and make new friends. Placing on top of that a label can really add to the stress they feel.

This singling out is not meant to be harmful, rather it is meant to be protective. For instance, in the United States some schools institute "allergy tables" at lunch, where kids with allergies must sit together (or sometimes alone). This practice is in place to keep children with allergies safe, but ultimately is stigmatizing. So navigating with schools requires a balance that protects your child from both allergic reaction and from feeling different.

Living overseas gives us the opportunity to work alongside schools to try and strike that balance; however, as we have tried to do this we have struggled with feeling like we were going at it alone without resources or support that we likely would have in the U.S.

In Malawi we had a few other surprises while working with the school. For instance, the locally hired school nurse had never administered an EpiPen, nor had she ever even seen one! My husband ended up doing a training for all the faculty on how to use an EpiPen that year, and then every year after that until we left Malawi.

We were also surprised by the amount of concern and interest that both expats and locals in Malawi had for our daughter's allergy. Although the clinical education and exposure to people with allergies was much lower than what we encountered in the United States, the people of Malawi asked more questions in an attempt to understand our needs. This was very encouraging for us.

Since that first instance using an EpiPen on our three-year-old, we then had five years of carrying around EpiPens without needing to use them. That's not to say we didn't have a few scares. We had numerous overseas "exposures" that raised our heart rates a bit but ultimately did not require an Epi. There was the time Alex was given a peanut butter cup by a friend, the "safe" granola bar that made her mouth itch, the swollen face and itchy eyes after a bite of a classmate's birthday party cupcakes which used peanut flour, the gourmet pesto pizza that substituted peanuts in the pesto since they ran out of pine nuts, the school performance where the cast threw peanuts into the audience, the teacher who ate a peanut butter sandwich in the teachers' lounge and then simply breathed near Alex. The list goes on and on.

It wasn't until Alex was eight years old that we had to use an EpiPen again. This time we were living in Mozambique. We were at a going-away party for one of our embassy colleagues, with a buffet dinner catered by a local restaurant. The fact that the menu contained all of the traditional foods was initially lost on me. I made plates of food for my kids onto which I put some bland, kid-friendly looking items. Alex took one bite and knew — "Mom, my mouth is hurting." What I thought was creamed spinach was actually the Mozambican traditional dish, *matapa*, which is full of pureed peanuts — a dish I had been actively avoiding for one and a half years. Because of the avoidance, I had no idea what it looked like, and instead of stumbling through a conversation in my lackluster Portuguese, I didn't inquire with anyone about the menu. I let my guard down; in fact, my guard was pretty non-existent as I didn't even have an EpiPen with me. My mistake meant my daughter could have died.

Luckily, the reaction was mild and slow this time. We took her home and watched her, and when it was clear she was struggling to breathe, we gave her the shot. Now I know that not speaking the local language is no excuse for being less vigilant — it was clear to me that I have to communicate more, and never assume all is safe, as it could be the difference between life and death for my daughter.

Our overseas incidents make me wonder if it would be easier to live in the United States with a child who has a life-threatening allergy. For instance, students in the U.S. have 504 plans with their schools; these are detailed plans developed in collaboration with physicians, parents, and the school systems that provide a framework that guides how the school will handle a child's allergy. This legally binding document provides individualized standard procedures for the school, which helps give peace of mind to the families and clarity to the schools.

While some of the allergy experience may be specific to living overseas, other aspects seem universal. I follow a Facebook thread for U.S. and Canadian families managing food allergies, and there are a lot of the same concerns as I have. Parents talk about diligence with food ingredients, travel preparations, how sometimes food allergies are not taken seriously by other parents or family members, and the pain of children being singled out, or even bullied or discriminated against. On the other hand, the group members also share lovely stories of people going above and beyond to insure the child never feels "less than" and who get that allergies can be life-or-death issues. One advantage to being overseas is that our expat communities tend to really come together for one another, and we possibly encounter more of these amazingly supportive people as expats than we would living in the U.S.

The childhood I experienced was one where I went to school with the same children for most of my life and where I knew the families in my community since I could remember. The expat lifestyle means you are constantly meeting new people, traveling to new places and exploring new things. As the parent of a child with severe allergies living in an environment where everything is new and unknown, I have to be vigilant all the time. I have to try harder to learn at least some of the local language, to understand how the culture understands allergies, and to feel comfortable with accessing medical care. I have to balance being taken seriously with being considered over protective. Living overseas adds a few layers to challenges that parents in their familiar environments face. It may not be the lifestyle choice for others who have loved ones with severe allergies, and it may seem like a lot of work and worry, but it was the right choice for us.

Barbara Singer embraced the adventures and anxieties of moving overseas almost seven years ago. Since that time she has mastered driving a diesel 6-speed on the left hand side of the road and haggling at local markets, but continues to fail miserably in learning foreign languages and contending with large insects. As a trailing spouse, global health professional, cancer survivor, and mom of three, Barbara's mantra is "Don't let perfect be the enemy of good."

Looking Forward: Discovering Europe with Lyme Disease, My Wheelchair ... and Gusto

By Mary M. Al-Akhdar

We did not ask for this room or this music. We were invited in. Therefore, because the dark surrounds us, let us turn our faces to the light. Let us endure hardship to be grateful for plenty. We have been given pain to be astounded by joy. We have been given life to deny death. We did not ask for this room or this music. But because we are here, let us dance.

Stephen King, 11/22/63

I recently realized that in my dreams, I am never in a wheelchair. I remember being five years old, having no thoughts or worries about taking care of myself — when a summer day meant spreading a blanket in the backyard to practice handstands and backbends, playing badminton in the street with my father until it got dark out, and putting fireflies in mason jars until the grass stains on my bare feet were so thick that my mother insisted it was bath time.

When I first became handicapped, I was like the proverbial frog immersed in water, not noticing the changes in water temperature as it heats to a slow boil. As I lost my health, I didn't notice my life changing. I didn't notice myself looking for the ramps up every sidewalk, seeking fitting rooms with a chair to sit in, noting department stores I would eventually avoid because they offered no respite, until I rarely left my home because dressing exhausted me. We then purchased my first wheelchair. I don't always need it, but if anything requires the slightest strength and stamina, it is a must. How did I get to that place? It is enough to say that an undiagnosed tick bite can transform your life.

But I've found, over the years, that life exists in balance, for those who look up from time to time. And in my early 40s, my husband and three daughters and I moved to Switzerland for an employment opportunity. We had been living on the Gulf Coast of the U.S., in Mobile, Alabama. Flat, hot, and ever so familiar. At that time in my life, I might have been dreaming of the past, but I was about to look forward.

It is now ten years after that move, and we are back in the U.S., but remembrances of living in Europe still fill me up. For instance, I reflect on our memorable trip to Rome. We visited Rome three weeks before Christmas 2010. We had booked that trip just before riots broke out in Rome, students protesting cuts in education funding. It was calm when we arrived, but we were warned that another "uprising" was planned for that evening and to stay away from central Rome where the crowds were to gather.

Our first obstacle to getting around was the 2,000-year-old cobblestone roadways crusted over with shattered ice and flakes of snow. Large, slippery reddish cobblestones with worn-down spaces separating them are not hospitable to a wheelchair. Bumpety bumpety my wheelchair struggled, stopped, jarred and twisted. My family of five threw glances all around. Where was the first ramp off these cobblestones and onto a sidewalk? Finding one required a hunt.

Of course, being in Rome meant an attempt to see the Coliseum. Our guide spoke English and took me to the elevators as we moved around levels of the arena, directing the bipeds to meet her at our destination. Her English was embellished by her Italian accent, a short vowel sound at the end of each word, her sentences pleasantly undulating from one word to the next: "The marble of the original-a Coliseum-a was removed in later-a years-a for making of-a monuments-a and fountains-a." My ears were working hard. She held the handles behind my wheelchair while she delivered her memorized facts.

I was grateful to be off the cobblestones while we viewed the Coliseum. Being in a wheelchair, I could not roam where the gladiators once prepared for a possible death, but I looked down on the exposed quadrants that were at one time below ground, with irregularly worn-down stone walls, as my family explored them, running around what was now an open maze, laughing in quarters that long ago made men pray for mercy.

Near the Coliseum was the Forum, a long expanse of Roman remains, stepping-stones, fallen columns, and once glorious sculptures and temples, now scattered around a rough, barren-earth terrain. A wheelchair could not navigate this site; the wheels could not move without falling into some pit or having to conquer some large stone. Our daughters decided to go along with the tour group, and my husband stayed behind with me, heartbroken that I could not participate. But he had an idea. There was a "lift" that could lower a person into the ending point of the Forum (why would that ever be necessary?). He asked for help to lower me and my wheelchair into the Forum, which we succeeded in doing. His plan was that we would see how far towards the tour group we could get and then backtrack with the group once we met up with them.

That sounded all well and good, but once lowered into the Forum, no effort could move my wheelchair through the dirt and rock. Push and jar and tip, and all we did was stay in the same place, laughing at our own hopelessly naïve plans. When the tour met us at the tail end of the Forum, we exited the site as a family and shared stories of our escapades, and lack thereof.

We rolled through the city, searching for the nearest ramp onto a sidewalk, until at one point the search ended with us finding a ramp that was blocked at the sidewalk level by a rotating postcard stand. I could see the tension in my husband's shoulders after realizing that the store owner found the sale of postcards more important than accessibility for the disabled. My husband picked up the postcard display in one fell swoop and planted it in the front of the store. He came back and rolled me up onto the sidewalk, and then he pivoted at a right angle and walked determinedly into the establishment. My daughters and I had the same thought simultaneously. With one daughter behind me pushing and two leading the sprint, we moved swiftly away from the potential "instruction" my husband might offer the employees!

By nightfall, taxi drivers started to warn us to stay off the main path, as student protesters might be as violent as the week before, so we headed for side streets and their enticing little shops of lace, antiques, jewelry, and religious paraphernalia. Before we got far, we had a problem once again. The military was out that night to contain the protesters to a certain area, and a side street we wanted to traverse was blocked by a tank, literally. It was parked sideways, preventing us from making our usual bumpety-bumpety way down the ice-encrusted cobblestones. With great indignation, my husband pushed my chair up to a soldier and pointed out using both English and gestures, that his tank was in our way. I was considering our own audacity to assume that our shopping should not be prevented by a city crisis, when a soldier looked down at me in my chair and hopped into his tank to move it for us, apologizing in Italian over and over: "*Mi dispiace!*" My husband and I could not find the words at that moment, nor our children! But I do remember nodding to them while heading down that side street, our family unit sneaking glances at each other while keeping our heads straight forward.

I often reflect on my lot in life, needing these wheels as I do because of the undiagnosed tick bite and its repercussions. But I have experienced this loss with a heaping dose of self-will, nurtured by my family's fierce solidarity and determination that I shouldn't be limited. Europe gave me the opportunity to experience great joy, from sources as unlikely as a soldier manning his tank — even though my wheelchair still wobbles today from the after-effects of the large, worn, ice-encrusted cobblestones of Rome.

When we moved to Switzerland in 2007, three years before that powerful visit to Rome, the removal of impediments to fully functional and independent life for the handicapped was just being undertaken. A national Disability Equality Act (*Behindertengleichstellungsgesetz*) had been implemented in 2004, and work had begun to make all existing public buildings accessible to the disabled. New private buildings were also to be constructed disabled-accessible, unless exempt for certain conditions.

While Europe was still learning how to build appropriate spaces for people with disabilities, living in the U.S. had given me advantages I didn't know how to live without. Many American shopping communities appear to be mostly made up of parking lots, with big spaces for our oversized, gas-guzzling vehicles (try putting your wheelchair into a Mazda3 and getting it out in tight European parking). I was accustomed to the many handicapped parking spaces in front of every store and ramps onto every sidewalk and into every public place. Even bathrooms were accommodating. What would I find in Europe?

Upon arriving in Switzerland, our first big decision affected by my disability was where we should live in a land where locals seldom drove. Mass transit was the norm. And many destinations had no parking whatsoever. The most crucial requirement then was proximity to mass transit. I had to be able to get to a bus or tram by myself. And, the terrain between my home and the transit stop had to be flat (in Switzerland!), and not so long that it was intimidating to attempt.

It was at this point in my life that I first honed my skills at assessing how many meters an expanse of road appeared to be. Our temporary apartment was, I remember, 80 meters from the tram stop closest to us. And the road was flat. This distance I could walk at that time, but not much farther. After three months of searching, I was especially lucky to find a one-level apartment, less than 80 meters from a bus stop, also offering ample underground parking. Jackpot!

Next task: getting a driver's license and a handicapped decal. This involved an appointment with the driver-testing officials, where my husband and I presented my doctor's paperwork describing my limitations and had to answer many questions: "On a good day, can you walk one kilometer? How often do you use your car? Are you able to drive standard? How often do you anticipate using handicapped parking?"

What I didn't see coming was the physical test done in the licensing offices. Raised on a platform across from the interviewer's desk sat a very small "idea" of a vehicle, something perhaps that Fred Flintstone might have found state-of-the-art. It was red, as I remember, the body of a car with no wheels — a steering wheel and pedals inside and nothing more. They needed to test the speed of my physical reaction to a crisis — how long it would take me to slam on the brakes, and how hard I could slam them. As it was explained to me, getting a disability decal was not just a benefit. They must also be sure I was not a danger to others on the road. This possibility had not crossed my mind before, but it struck me as an obvious concern.

I had to sit in the red "vehicle," interviewer sitting next to me with a stopwatch. As instructed, I pushed the green button on the "dashboard" to begin the simulated experience of driving, and when the interviewer coolly said "Stop" and simultaneously squeezed his watch, I had to hit the brake with enough force in as little time as possible, demonstrating a healthy reaction time. I'm sad to say, it took me three tries to meet the requirement for licensing. The testing official reacted kindly when I failed the first two tries, with a collected, focused and softly spoken request to please try again, while taking a deep breath as if to coach me to stay calm. I felt he was rooting for me.

And then one final question: "Is your left leg weaker than your right? Are you as strong when driving manual?" Instantly realizing my answer could lead to restrictions on my license, I gave a firm answer — my left leg was fine and I had no trouble with manual, thank you. I was granted a handicap decal that day. But as the interviewer shook my hand to conclude our session, he left me with one final direction: "Please don't use the handicapped spaces if you are having a good day. There aren't that many of them."

And indeed, there are not. But I did use them frequently, especially if running into the grocery for a few items all alone, when no one could rescue me if I were shopping on foot and realized I did not have the ability to walk back to my car.

On one sunny Swiss day, I went into a large shopping market for bread, cheese — the usual staples. The song "Flight of the Bumble Bee" buzzed in my head as I knew my ability to walk was waning, so I needed to shop quickly. Upon returning to the parking lot, I had to pay the fee for my parking ticket before heading to my car. And much to my dismay with my sinking strength, I did not have the right change for the machine. I stood there with my grocery bag at my feet, aware that a man was standing behind me, waiting his turn. What to do?

I turned around and took in the Swiss man behind me. Did he have kind eyes? Would he give me correct change? And what if he didn't speak English? Am I to be stuck in the parking lot? (High anxiety!) I asked him and he gladly gave me the change, his English nearly as good as mine. He then wanted to help me to my car. I accepted. He slung my cloth shopping bag over his shoulder and started in with the general questions, assuming we would have to walk some distance to my vehicle. Sweat had already begun to bead on my forehead from persevering through my physical pain with the usual grace and silence.

"So, what brought you to Switzerland? How long will you be staying? Do you find you like it here?" All the questions the expats agreed we should print t-shirts with the answers on.

But before I could answer a single question, we were standing right in front of my car, in the handicapped parking spot. I stopped. When he realized we were at our destination in a matter of 10 meters, he looked at me with great concern. The timbre of his voice became softer. With paced-out words, he asked me, "Do you know what those painted lines are on this parking spot? Do you know what that picture in the middle of the spot is for?" All of this said in the gentlest of manners, assuming my complete innocence, new to his country.

I smiled momentarily while contemplating his bluntly cut, softly waving blond hair, his blue eyes, and his gentle spirit, and then gave a controlled response. "Yes. It's a handicapped parking spot. I'm handicapped." I knew from years of experience that explaining my full situation had no short version.

With more than the usual pause before speaking, he suddenly realized what he had said to me — that he had assumed that nothing in my life could prevent me from parking farther away, when in fact, he could not see my disability. I observed the realization settle on him as every muscle in his face turned a bit downward. He didn't know what else to say. I can say he was kind.

The invisible illness of Lyme disease and co-infections is mysterious to anyone without the burden of living with it. Having it quickly brings on isolation. Pain and malaise are not its only calling cards, but also neurological and cognitive problems, such as brain fog and issues with word retrieval and short-term memory. For an expat, this means that learning a new language can be even more challenging than usual. My language classes were an exercise in frustration and humiliation, combined with the stress of easing three daughters into a new culture and keeping a home with "no fuel in my tank." I knew I was smart; I knew the material was in my brain, but I couldn't find the "folder" and pull it out, so to speak. But it could have been much worse, considering that the greater Basel, Switzerland, area had an estimated 30,000 expats, most of whom had English in common, and the many locals who studied English in school.

Nevertheless, not knowing the language required very creative techniques for finding items in the grocery store. I would ask if a person spoke English, using my little bit of German: "*Sprechen Sie Englisch?*"

"*Nein*," was usually the answer.

O.K. I would then try to point to pictures on different products, thinking my grocery store victim might magically realize that I was talking about a recipe (I'm generally a hopeful person), and then I'd pantomime the one ingredient I couldn't find. In this way, a young male store clerk stood in front of me while I acted out making cake, including the motion of a bowl in my arms and breaking eggs, stirring, and then me saying, "flour?" (I know, no need to say it.) Eventually the young man looked relieved and pointed to the flowers at the front of the store. I guess I didn't care what anyone thought of me; it was a matter of feeding the family! I thanked him, "*Danke*," and continued to scan grocery shelves until I found flour, or "*Mehl*," a word that I immediately added to my vocabulary.

On another occasion, I got much luckier. I was searching for glass cleaner and stood in front of a great row of cleaning products. At first glance, they all looked the same to me. I asked my question to an elderly lady near me: "*Sprechen Sie Englisch?*"

"*Nein.*"

I waved my hand across the long row of cleaning products and shrugged my shoulders. This I followed by making a fist with each hand just below my eyeglass rims and pointing my index fingers straight up across the lenses. Then I made the two fingers move back and forth, simultaneously and in the same direction, across the front of my lenses, like windshield wipers.

The elderly lady jumped up and down like she had come up with the winning answer on a game show and pointed to a cleaner near the end of the shelf. As I peered closer to the bottle. I saw a picture of sparkling glass. Then it was my turn to jump up and down. The lady and I parted ways with me feeling like it was a truly successful day.

All this was not to say that I wasn't shamed from time to time by a local or two. For example, one fall afternoon in the grocery, I tried locating sauerkraut. As I stood in the aisle with pickles, olives and vinegar, I saw no sauerkraut, nor could I remember the word kraut. A local woman, statuesque, well dressed and accessorized, was standing there too. I caught her eye and said *"Guten Tag,"* the common Swiss greeting for "good day."

"Sprechen Sie Englisch?" I asked her. *"Nein,"* she answered ... after a pause. I felt her heavy silence further shackle my brain in the busy grocery store. "It is warm in here," I thought. Under her gaze, I started to wish I had worn newer shoes ... and perhaps lipstick!

I decided to lurch into my pantomime formula to find the necessary food item. I pointed to pickles, but how in the world would a person gesture cabbage? Perplexed at how to pull this off, my hands moved towards each other unconsciously, as if to mold something round. I started a "chop chop chop" motion with my right hand and murmured softly, "sour cabbage, how do I say sour cabbage?"

She quickly answered me, in a flat voice with rather good English, "Cabbage is not in season; you won't find it."

So she did know English! She walked away with dignity,

gliding in unison with her shopping cart and in no hurry to leave me behind. She had let me stand there, pointing, molding and chopping the air to pieces, and had no desire to rescue me. She delivered the stinger while remaining in her comfort zone.

It was later that day that I remembered the word *kraut*, a word I had used many times in the past. My paternal grandparents were of Germanic origin, my grandmother from Austria-Hungary before the Great War. Kraut was served often in our home when I was growing up. But with the cognitive difficulties, memory and word retrieval problems of Lyme disease, the folder containing the word sauerkraut was tucked far into the folds of my brain. I could not find it, much less open it.

After that incident, I knew I had to retire the point-and-pantomime method for grocery shopping. I'm not always going to find sympathy. I bathed, once again, in the knowledge that I had little control over this thing that could bring me public shame, this problem with learning a new language while in the grips of tick-borne illness. I knew trying to explain what others could not see as my handicap was insurmountable. The language issue was a daily companion, but one I decided to wade through, if not gracefully, then with full self-esteem. In public.

Despite the struggles with language, mobility was a greater issue for me. I wanted to get around, see things, experience places. And living in Switzerland posed continual transport challenges for me. Anytime I wanted to leave my house alone, I would evaluate my ability to do so by deciding if I could get to that bus stop 50 meters away. And once I got there and escaped my apartment, would I be able to return to the bus stop and walk back to the apartment? For this reason, I would often take the car from the parking garage beneath the apartment. I had found two parking decks that had good tram stops just outside. One was outside the city of Basel, under a nice shopping center close to the children's school. I could park there and hop on the tram just outside the shops, getting back to the car in time to collect my children from school and drive us all home. Parking at this place cost far less than at any parking deck in the city.

But within my first year, I heard from other American moms who had taken to parking beneath this shopping center "just because" (American expectation for convenience) that the property owners had noticed from their security camera footage that people were parking there for long afternoons. This is a habit that is highly frowned upon in any Swiss situation. Their culture demands that people walk, bike or take the tram or bus to destinations. Taking up a parking spot belonging to a business was just plain frivolous and not to be tolerated. From then on, cars were given citations for parking beyond the short time established for shopping.

I had to find an alternative parking deck, but the next best thing was a downtown garage that allowed all-day parking. Parking an entire afternoon to get around town and conveniently jump on a tram or bus put a hole in the budget, if done regularly. And if someone took me downtown or anywhere in my wheelchair, the issue was getting on and off trams, wheeling up and down cobblestone streets with steep inclines, and finding bathrooms a wheelchair could access.

At times, when leaving the apartment, I felt like Sisyphus of Greek mythology, rolling his stone up the hill, only to have it roll back on him. The effort for me to get somewhere was enough to send me right back home. On the other hand, the built-in understanding of the Swiss and other Europeans was commendable. Some tram stops had markings for the spot where a wheelchair should wait for the tram, the tram stopping in exactly the right place for the wheelchair to have a lesser bump-up wheelie to enter the vehicle. And if necessary, the tram driver would hop out — and this had to be done quickly as trams were ALWAYS on time — and put out a metal ramp. The effort of those running the infrastructure was quite gallant.

Yet it was a significant investment of time and networking with friends to find public bathrooms on ground level or with elevator access. Most older buildings, which were the majority in this historic city, had bathrooms down a narrow, winding staircase in the basement.

What other difficulties did a wheelchair encounter? Well, many streets preserved the legacy of medieval towns, with little "aqueducts" or "street gutters" running down the middle of the road, rather than at the sides, to carry the water away. For a wheelchair to cross, it had to maneuver the cement gully of water separating one side of the street from the other. I found that it wasn't that hard: find a little bridge over the water, get to the other side, and find a ramp onto the sidewalk. Then, search for a store that did not involve a huge curb to enter, and you were home free!

All these impediments to mobility might sound overwhelming, but the human factor almost never let me down. When we visited Barcelona, the Gaudi Cathedral had very steep ramps to enter, as the initial design had not taken handicap access into consideration. I always knew when my husband was struggling behind me to get my wheelchair up a very steep ramp. I pictured him practically horizontal to the ground as he leaned forward to push. And then I would ask him tensely while still looking straight ahead, "Are you horizontal again?" thinking it was time to feel embarrassed. And he would give a reluctant "yes." While I felt myself shrinking in my chair, a stranger would suddenly grab hold of one of the wheelchair arms and tug while my husband pushed, and I would be released from gravity, moving swiftly to the entrance of a building. My husband would then stand upright, hands gripping his lower back as he arched into a glorious stretch. Notably, these sudden angel-strangers rarely lingered for us to thank them. It seemed that knowing "the right thing to do" was inherent in mankind, on a widespread basis.

There were even special moments when the beauty of the experience was directly bound to my wheelchair. I remember visiting Torino, Italy, in May 2010. The Shroud of Turin was on display again after a long hiatus from public view. Upon buying tickets for the viewing, I had been prompted to state if I needed handicap assistance, to which I, of course, said yes. Heading for the cathedral, wheelchair necessary, we rounded one city block after another, our pack of five scanning our surroundings to enhance our visual experience. As we turned another corner, the cathedral came into view, and we gasped! The crowds waiting to get into the building to view the Shroud spanned many city blocks, with people from around the globe — Coptic priests, Saudis in their robes, Buddhists and everything in between.

How, I thought, would I have my turn? And then, while circling the cathedral's enclosed grounds, we found a rusted iron gate with a white placard on it that said "Handicap" in many languages. A light-hearted elderly gentleman welcomed my family onto the cathedral grounds through this decrepit, tilted gate that scraped the ground and screeched when it wobbled opened and shut. Though the man was of slight build, he insisted on pushing my wheelchair through the crowds. He pushed me up the long, steep wooden ramp to the cathedral entrance, insisting that everyone in line make way, my family following close behind, as if I were in my chariot and the Red Sea was parting for me alone. Before I knew it, we were inside, but below ground level, swiftly gliding along musty, tan-colored stone corridors, with side corridors springing up here and there at right angles. (I had the feeling that if we were to be abandoned below the cathedral, finding a way out could prove elusive.)

Then what did I hear? My family and I looked at each other ... Gregorian Chant? Yes, it was, but coming from what corridor ... or every corridor? I had goosebumps as I imagined I had entered a fourth dimension, some "other-worldly" place, my wheelchair gliding through the musty sunless world of stone and floating choir chants.

We ascended to ground level and natural light, to the pre-room that held the next group to visit the Shroud. When the doors opened to the darkened room of the Shroud, my heart sank at the number of people ahead of me. In my wheelchair, I would never see a thing. But then I was swung ahead of the group by the slightly built gentleman and slipped into place in front of the rail that held the crowds away. While the masses stood behind me, behind the rail, I was as close to the sight as one could be, in a line-up of elderly people also in wheelchairs. When the Shroud was illuminated, I was overcome. My family was directly behind me, just behind the rail. I looked to them tearfully; they beamed at me, at my joy.

Seeing the Mona Lisa at the Louvre was like seeing the Shroud of Turin. There was the throng of people packed behind a rail, keeping them safely out of touching distance of the painting. But I was wheeled in front of the rail by museum employees, again with my family directly behind me, behind the rail. By this time, my fear of missing the sight of something had lessened, thanks to many experiences of handicap protocols in public places.

Many happy thoughts of living in Europe are indelible in my mind. Europe is bountiful with potential experiences, history, structures and streets a thousand years old. I think of my life in Europe as life "condensed." Ancient buildings and the great expanse of history heighten the experience of simply turning a doorknob at, say, Versailles. Did Marie Antoinette touch it too? What lowly worker laid the centuries-old cobblestones beneath my feet or wheels? What stonemasons and sculptors prepared the many chiseled holy images in the Strasbourg Cathedral? How many other lives intertwined with my own to weave this tapestry of history, stretching from long ago to far into the future?

I felt part of life, and it part of me. My chest swelled with possibility and yearned for my next experience. I was alive: I was looking forward. I wanted to dance — and dance I did — to the exhilarating, bumpety-bump rhythm of life. I had my dance partners: my handicap, my wheelchair, my family, and many European vistas. There was music everywhere.

Former university English teacher and magazine editor Mary Al-Akhdar is a dedicated writing coach and editor, and a lover of the arts, her family, and the planet we live on. She adores the aesthetic experience, whether musical, visual, or written. She currently lives in Cary, N.C., where she is carving out a life once again after repatriating from Switzerland.

Kolkata: The Veil of the Real

By L. York

It is that time of the morning when my senses are just coming online. My eyes are still closed, but I sense the sun is up. I start to hear sounds. Birdsong, cars, water running, the general hum of life. This particular morning, I hear the birdsong first. I'm not coming out of any dream in particular, but I just have a sense of soft contentment and anticipation of an enjoyable day. Then my ears refine the birdsong. I'm hearing a harsh song. A crow song. My contentment dissipates. I'm left with a tightness around my stomach as if someone just put a vise grip on it. It hits me. I'm not in my bed. I'm not in my home. The bed is hard and harsh like the birdsong. I'm on the other side of the world, in a foreign land. I'm in Kolkata, India.

What brought us to this side of the world was my wife. It was her (our) first assignment coming out of her U.S. Foreign Service training class. The first diplomatic assignment is announced in a ceremony known as Flag Day, as the newly trained diplomat is called to the stage to receive a small flag of the country he/she will be sent to. It's one of those memories that always sticks with you. Not for the pomp and circumstance, but for the unique mix of anticipation, anxiety, relief, excitement.

I'm the type of person who has limited expectations and minimal hopes of how things will be. I've learned that a healthy amount of pragmatism and skepticism always buffers you against the disappointments that are a part of life. Being assigned to Kolkata was not a disappointment, but a big unknown. I wasn't sure what to expect.

The unexpected wasn't completely foreign terrain for me. I had started my adventures in the unexpected early in my life. I was the first in my family to go to college, the first to get a master's degree, the first to live in a big city (Washington, D.C.), and the first in my family to entertain the idea that the difficulties in life could be dealt with by something other than alcohol. I had completed a yoga teacher training course, and I had been working for an innovative and well-connected nonprofit in the integrative health care space. I had an amazing work family and a lively and fun life outside of work, and life in general was on a pretty even keel.

It was at this point in 2009 that my wife looked at me and stated she thought she was meant to be a Foreign Service Officer. To be honest, I had to research what that meant. I learned that the high school Model United Nations I participated in, where I traveled to New York City and served as the representative for Thailand and Oman, was the mirror of what the State Department did in other countries. We would be the ones to travel to the consulates and embassies outside our home country. Thus began my book learning of what it would mean to be a Foreign Service family.

I emphasize the book learning aspect because to this day

there is no real way to prepare for the Foreign Service except for being in it. Reading and talking to people who were in the Foreign Service gives you a rational, theoretical view of Foreign Service life. I knew that things would change. I knew we would be living in another country, but what did that actually mean? What did being a Foreign Service spouse mean? I had no real-life experience that could accurately answer these questions.

Up until this point the closest thing my wife did that resembled following each other's careers and moving to a foreign land was when my wife agreed to indulge my wish to work on films before I died. In 2003 we sold our condo, moved to New York City, and bounced around Brooklyn where I worked on films and she pursued her dream of being on Broadway. It was a mutually agreed-upon adventure. We both weren't expecting anything from it. We were in our 20s, no commitments (except to each other), and had plenty of money from the sale of our condo. Life was an adventure for both of us.

I would like to say I was supporting my wife in her pursuit of her "dream job," but that wouldn't be the truth. I never felt like the Foreign Service life was a choice for me. It was a choice for my wife, and I went along with it with no idea what the ride was going to be like. I had even less of an idea of what India was going to be like and how I would respond in such a completely foreign environment. Therein lay the issue — I agreed to something, but I had no idea what that something was.

Again, I'm a researcher at heart and by professional training, but all the typical research was of no help to me when we set foot in India.

I read about India. I talked with other Foreign Service spouses. I went to the Foreign Service Institute's library of information about diplomatic postings. I attended the "Intro to Foreign Service Life" workshop in Washington, D.C. I was in this weird space where I was still well entrenched in my current life and reading up on what my new life was going to be. I felt like I was blindly preparing for a major life experience.

My current employer was willing to keep me on part-time as a consultant, but that was not going to be enough income for us, so I also applied and signed on for one of the part-time jobs at the Consulate that Foreign Service spouses could do. This didn't really appeal to me, but it was going to be something to do. Something that put me in touch with other Americans on a regular basis. So I had all the bases covered — a new job, the amenities we heard were hard to procure in India, domestic help lined up, and a plan to bring our Pomeranian to post once we arrived.

We started investigating cars and learning where our apartment was and what might be around it according to Google Maps. In my mind, I was prepared, yet I cannot properly express how unprepared I was for India — for all of it.

I wasn't prepared for the sensory onslaught I experienced as soon as we left the plane. My nose tussled with the competing smells — none of which smelled familiar or pleasant. My eyes were overwhelmed with the scene — feral dogs and cats running around, a visual crush of humanity, the visible pollution, and the looks. It was like being in a fishbowl.

Nothing prepares you for the fascination that comes from being a white Westerner in this part of the world. The sounds were a cacophony of chatter, car horns, engines, and yelling. The sheer volume of people constantly pressing on me. The beggars pushing up to me because in this part of the world the color of my skin equaled wealth.

In retrospect the sensory onslaught could be equated with a symptom of an underlying problem. The underlying problem I would grapple with for the next year was — who was I in this new world?

Back in the U.S. I was not just a spouse. I was a budding researcher, I was a fierce friend, I was steady, I was engaging, I was funny, my life was structured and I knew my role in it. Even better, I knew what to do when it got tough. I had my coffee shop, I had my yoga class, I had a movie to go to, a bookstore to tuck into, I had a million varied food options, and I could run outside on trails, on roads, or play basketball. I could watch all my favorite events of the year — the NCAA basketball tournament, the World Series, and the Oscars. I could decompress with numerous people and converse about culturally shared experiences. I had a purpose that fit how I saw myself, who I thought I was, and how I wanted people to see me.

Now all that was gone. I was completely disoriented. Untethered and with no compass to help me orient myself. Plus all the things I doubled down on — the job at the Consulate, holding onto my old job even in a part-time capacity, and all the food amenities we had put into our household shipment— didn't serve me well in adjusting to this new life.

I became angry, disengaged, and a borderline alcoholic. I didn't recognize myself. Worst of all, I hated myself. I hated myself for being weak in the face of all the change and unevenness; I hated myself for being mean to my wife and to myself, and for just not being able to slap myself out of the funk I had sunk into.

Disguising my drinking became a sport for me. It was as if that was the thing I was really good at. I wouldn't drink all day every day, but I would on a number of weekdays start drinking in the afternoon. I would down one to two gin and tonics before 5 p.m. and then drink with my wife during dinner. That would provide a solid buzz for the later half of my day and into the evening.

It was also as if the drinking was draining any empathy I should have had for my wife. She was in a new country, new job, new culture too, yet somehow when I drank, I didn't care. All I had the capacity for was my own struggle. I would just keep thinking of reasons of why she had it better. She got to go to work. She got to work in a substantive job (as opposed to the dull, low-valued part-time work I soon abandoned), and was able to socialize with other Americans during the day; and most bitingly, she had a purpose.

I would like to say there was some lightning-bolt moment that changed everything around for me, but there wasn't. Real life is not a movie. We don't just experience a montage and come out okay on the other side. Life is an endeavor; it is like Leonard Cohen wrote: "It's a cold and it's a broken Hallelujah." That is what I did in that first year in Kolkata, I endeavored to dig myself out of a rock I had put myself under. It wasn't Kolkata that was crushing me. I can only say this in retrospect, but Kolkata was a gift. More on that later.

My time in Kolkata was not a straight line. Much like the roads in Kolkata, it was winding, filled with potholes, no guideposts, destination unknown, and bursting with life all along the way. The potholes were sometimes craters.

Besides the drinking, what also didn't help was the complete isolation I felt — self-imposed — and my rejection of any help. I didn't want to be told what to do to help myself. I come from a very self-reliant family. Depending on people was always a weakness, and crying in front of people was practically a sin. What was also sinful was talking about what I was struggling with in any real way. Talking with someone when I was drunk — while not acceptable — was understandable.

My defenses were down.

So there I was. One booze-filled, anger-laden year down and another one on the horizon and I still had not successfully figured out how to help myself cope. Toward the end of that first year my wife would receive one of the best bits of advice from another Foreign Service Officer: the one-month, three-month rule. Every month get out of Kolkata — whether it be in another part of the state of West Bengal or another part of India, it didn't matter — just get out of Kolkata. Then every three months get out of the country.

We didn't follow this rule exactly, but we did begin to travel. That was the crack in the proverbial rock I had crawled under. Our first major trip out of Kolkata was to Kerala. However, it wasn't just going to Kerala that started to shift something in me. It was the book I brought with me that was given to me by my friend, titled "Mindfulness in Plain English."

Always a fan of being by water, I sat by the Indian Ocean every day we were in Kerala and devoured that book.

That book reminded me of what I had completely forgotten from my yoga teacher training — my life wasn't as out of control as it seemed. My thoughts were totally normal, my reactions were simply human, my approach to this new life didn't have to be so confrontational, so hard.

I returned to being an observer. I had lost sight of this skill from my yoga teacher time. Observation without judgment. What I observed was that I had always pinned who I was to what I did for a living and how others saw me. Both of those guideposts are shifting sand. I had also lost sight of how I dealt with stress — exercise and meditation.

So while in Kerala, my wife and I crafted a plan. We would try to get us moved to the Consulate grounds, and I would give up the Consulate job that I didn't enjoy so I would have time to pursue other interests.

This was the turning point in our tour. We moved to the Consulate grounds. I was embedded in housing with other Americans (vs. locals), I had access to a gym on the grounds so I didn't have to worry about what I was wearing to work out, and I could see my wife every day for lunch.

All of a sudden my sails started flapping — I could feel the wind again. These actions buoyed me and set me up for a much more rich and enjoyable second year. The other thing that I could not have anticipated having an impact on me was the turnover of Americans at the Consulate. The newcomers were all around our age and some of them struggled like I did, but others didn't. One of them made pizzas, another brewed beer, another hosted parties with loud American music, and yet another was a personal trainer who happily worked with me to get me back on the workout track. I had some American culture back. I had connection again. I felt tethered again. And finally, I felt like I could venture out.

In India, tea is a ritual best enjoyed with others over conversation. Kolkata has an amazing collection of *chai wallahs* (tea-sellers). Each stall is different and each chai wallah makes their chai differently. Some are black and acidic, some are milky, some are sweet, and some — like that offered by the *chai wallah* right outside the Consulate on the bustling street — were for me, the perfect mix of acidic, milky, and sweet.

I started to have a chai every day. More connection. I went on tours of the city. I befriended a local painter who indulged my interest in learning to paint. He helped me to find a style and to this day I cherish the friendship and conversation we shared during those painting sessions.

I befriended another local who introduced me to the club culture in Kolkata. These were the clubs once run by the Brits but now occupied by the higher-caste Indians. I shared many delicious plates of food over gin and tonics. I also had the best *momos* (a type of South Asian dumpling) I've ever had, in a hole-in-the-wall restaurant. I learned more about cricket and became a fan of it.

I finally stepped into the bustling world around me in

Kolkata, and I happily devoured it. I now was embracing life as it was instead of wishing it was different.

I would like to say the lesson of Kolkata was immediately apparent while I was living in Kolkata, but it wasn't. Many of the most precious gifts in life are never really recognized as such when they are first received. Kolkata offered me many gifts once I was ready to receive them. New ways of looking at life, a greater, deeper appreciation of all that I had, and a love for something foreign.

One of the more significant gifts it gave me was perspective. Going through the experience of Kolkata helped me to understand that even when I feel like I'm on shaky ground, or life feels overwhelming, that is all it is — a feeling. I don't have to react to it, indulge it, or placate it. It can just be, and I can keep myself steady while things swirl around me.

This gift would become invaluable to me two years after our tour in Kolkata.

In 2014 we welcomed the birth of our first son into the world. Only it wasn't a smooth welcome. My wife had to have an urgent C-section. Our son suffered a brain bleed when he was born. His bleed was so substantial and the damage severe enough that he had to be transferred to another hospital with a higher level NICU only eight hours after we were holding him. So for the first four days of his life I bounced from the hospital in which my wife was recovering to the other hospital where my son was being cared for by an amazing team of doctors and nurses. It remains one of the most emotionally and spiritually challenging times of my life. (Note: While the final outcome for our son — and anyone really — is yet to be determined, I can report that he is now a happy, love-filled, gregarious five-year-old.)

I often think that if I hadn't gone to Kolkata, experienced all that I had, re-learned who I am, and realized I could be steady in chaos, that I would have crumbled under the weight of this experience. To this day the things I learned about myself while in Kolkata continue to serve me and serve me well. That is the gift I was given in this Foreign Service life — it held up a mirror, challenged me to really see myself, accept myself with compassion and forgiveness, and embrace that which is different. I couldn't think of a better life lesson to carry forward and cherish.

L. York is the academic head of an acupuncture program outside of Washington, D.C. and has also served as a director for academic partnerships, establishing collaborative, integrative doctoral acupuncture internships at a leading behavioral health clinic. With an undergraduate degree in psychology and a Master of Science in physiology from Georgetown University, L. has also been involved in numerous research projects examining the effects of acupuncture for pain, stress, and PTSD in military and veteran populations. L. York is a parent to a gregarious 5-year-old boy who has cerebral palsy and a rambunctious 2-year-old. L's current focus is to leverage experience in the integrative health care space, research, and higher education to support a variety of initiatives within the cerebral palsy community.

Mindful in Madagascar

By Carolyn Parse and Jodi Harris

Note: Portions in bold are excerpts from Jodi's 2015 essay, When All You Can Do Is Breathe, *originally published on the Tiny Buddha website.*

"We decided long ago that we would never, ever, ever, EVER say we left Madagascar because Sam got Type 1 diabetes. It would always be … 'We left Madagascar because it doesn't have hospitals' like Madagascar was the problem. ….I never wanted him to feel like we gave something up because he got sick," explains Jodi Harris, mom to now 10-year-old Sam, 12-year-old Jasper, and six-year-old Imogen.

Founder of World Tree Coaching and a former clinical social worker, Jodi has authored two activity books for expats, including *Kids On the Move.* She knows about transitions, but these interactive resources don't necessarily reveal her intimate knowledge of the abrupt, complex, and unexpected passages that transform our lives seemingly overnight. Jodi is the mom of a Type 1 diabetic.

Every day is a series of ins and outs. We think things

should stay in a straight line, full speed ahead, but they don't. They go up and down. In and out.

Five years after Sam's diagnosis, they are living in Tokyo. Now they are all experts in carb-counting; Sam educates his international school community about Type 1 diabetes; and Jodi looks back with gratitude for the luck, learning, and love they've experienced along the way.

"It was a Sunday [in January] and we went to brunch at Café de la Gare — an old train station in Antananarivo — with 10 other families," she says. "They have a big outside area to play. We were all eating. It was a gorgeous summer day, so beautiful. We have so many pictures from that day. The kids were all running around, playing."

She's thoughtful, wistful, as she continues: "The community was really tight — [there was] a real commitment toward our friendships and building relationships. People pulled together instantly when there was a need."

As she fondly describes the details of a relaxed day with friends, Jodi recalls two odd behaviors in her then five-year-old. First, he ravenously cruised everyone's plates after they'd finished eating, and second, after gorging himself on leftovers, he curled up on his dad's lap and fell asleep.

Jodi describes Sam as seeming "under the weather" off and on over a period of a month or so. "My tummy hurts" or "My legs feel tired," he'd say. But these fleeting symptoms were easily explained away by friends as growing pains or the typical digestive disturbances commonplace in Madagascar.

"Everybody was always getting little sicknesses like worms or bacteria," Jodi explains. Every time her husband, Jeremy, left the capital for work, he'd return with some kind of illness.

Type 1 diabetes, also referred to as insulin-dependent diabetes or juvenile diabetes, is a chronic illness where the body's immune system destroys the insulin-making cells in the pancreas. With no insulin, the sugars in the blood build up and can cause life-threatening complications involving the eyes, kidneys, blood vessels, nerves, and heart.

The symptoms can be quite straightforward if you know what you're looking for, but in an environmental context where parasites and digestive disturbances are common and kindergartner complaints vague, the illness can fall under the radar, shrouded in misinterpretation.

In fact, it was four days after the brunch occurrence when Jodi received a call from the school that Sam was ill and needed to go home. When Jodi saw him, there were no symptoms that stood out. Nothing seemed to be wrong with him, she recalls.

The next day, Jodi dropped Sam off at a friend's house for a birthday party after school. When his dad picked him up, their friend Lourdes commented, "Sam was eating like crazy! He kept eating and eating and eating!" As Lourdes described the scene, Sam started throwing up in the driveway.

Later that evening while Jodi was preparing dinner, she caught Sam grabbing food from the fridge. "You just threw up, you're going to be sick!" she insisted. "But I'm so hungry!" he replied.

It wasn't until the next night that Jodi began to worry. She was scratching his back as she tucked him into bed. She likens the alarm she felt to what it might be like to find a lump in one's breast. "I could feel all his ribs and his whole spine," she says. "He's thin!" her brain shouted. "It's only been 48 hours and he's different." Her thoughts raced on, her heart creeping toward her throat.

She and Jeremy were just on their way out to join friends for a farewell dinner. Sam's odd behavior and weight loss became the main topic of discussion. Consensus was quickly reached: "You know it's worms ..." "I bet that's what it is!" "He's got a tapeworm," others regretfully chimed in. Jodi laughs at how run-of-the-mill that sounded at the time. These people had spent their entire careers in Africa. They were experts on the matter and probably right, she thought.

When they arrived home that night, the babysitter reported that Sam had been waking up and asking for food. She said she'd given him an apple and sent him back to bed, but "maybe something's wrong with him," she said on her way out.

When they woke the next morning, it became clear something was very wrong. They called the medical officer, "We can't keep him awake! He can't move. He can't walk!" The med officer quickly listed off a series of questions, "Has he been peeing a lot? Has he wet the bed? Does he look like he's lost weight? Has he been eating a lot?" When they answered yes to every question, he said, "It's Type 1 diabetes; I'm going to come and do the test, but it's Type 1 diabetes."

Jodi went straight to the computer and googled her anxiety higher. Type 1 diabetes is unpreventable, but treatable, attributed to genetics, environmental factors, and certain viruses. Right away, Jodi thought of her favorite uncle to whom her mother had donated a kidney when she was younger. He, too, had Type 1 diabetes and died at age 41.

For a child Sam's age, a normal blood sugar level would range somewhere between 80-200 milliliters per deciliter. When the medical officer tested Sam's blood sugar, it was off the chart, over 700. Sam was sleepy because he was slipping into a diabetic coma.

Jodi describes a "jittery" feeling that rises from her core as she recounts the circumstances around Sam's initial diagnosis. She feels cold, she says. It's chilling to remember how close they'd come to losing their "Buddha," the calm, easy-going, thoughtful one who kept them living in the moment.

I'd spent eighteen months in a place where I'd always feared one of my children would get sick or injured or worse. Eighteen months of saying, "Yes, it could happen, but it probably won't." Eighteen months out the window because now it was all happening. And we had to wait.

For those first few hours when my son's life was on the line, I had a moment of clarity. There was no time for doubt or self-judgment. The only anchor was his breath. And as his breath moved, and mine with it, we were fully absorbed in what was happening there in that moment.

When the embassy SUV arrived to transport them to the nearest version of a hospital, Jodi climbed in with her sleepy boy, in shock and fear, and kept moving. That would be the last time she'd see that house, the last time she'd see her other kids in Madagascar.

"Sam can't die. This isn't the story," she thought to herself as her brain caught up to her emotions.

Here I was beside him — breathing in and out. I don't even know when exactly it happened, but somehow the rest of the world began to fall away. We were just us, in that moment. The heavy weight of stress and fear and sadness and loss was with me, but all emotion existed in that moment alone. What was before seemed forever past, what was ahead faded into mystery. And there we were. Breathing. In and out.

When they arrived, the staff wanted to run their own tests while they hydrated him using a glucose (sugar) IV drip. Glucose is pure energy for the human body and often given to weak and dehydrated patients who are unable to take in calories through food. In Sam's case, however, glucose was exactly the opposite of what he needed at that moment.

Their medical officer didn't speak French. Suddenly, Jodi became medical liaison, cultural mediator, and translator. Her fear and sadness activated the ferocity within her. In French, she protested and persisted. "You think you're not capable of something, but you become so protective," she says, recalling how she insisted with medical staff until they agreed to use a saline solution instead to dilute the glucose and stress hormones in Sam's blood.

Jodi describes the emergency room like a closet with a

hospital bed. They kept losing power. "Ask them which type of insulin they're using," the med officer urged. But when she asked, they didn't seem aware that there were different types of insulin. Together, their level of confidence with Sam's medical treatment continued to plummet. He was finally stabilized, nonetheless.

I watched him breathe. In. Out. In. Out. Sometimes I'd move closer to his tiny body in his hospital bed just to see if I could get him to move a bit, wanting to boost the comfort of in and out with a roll to the side or an eye flicker.

This all reminded me of five years before, when he was a newborn and I'd do the same thing. You know about this if you're a parent or you've ever cared for an infant. Sometimes you just need to watch them breathe.

But of course now I was really watching my son to make sure he didn't die. In a few short days, he'd gone from seeming a bit under the weather to barely breathing. Now all of my greatest fears were being realized in the barely existent space between his body and mine. In and out. In and out.

Jeremy was home with the other two kids figuring out the next steps for them all. Their babysitter helped with baby Imogen, people brought food, friends helped Jasper get to and from school.

When the medevac was finally approved by the South African government and on its way, almost 18 hours later, Lourdes arrived with a travel bag for Jodi: two changes of clothes, toiletries, and a Kindle. In shock, Jodi repeated in Spanish, "Lourdes, I don't want to know this! I don't want to learn this!"

We made our way from the small, ill-equipped hospital in Antananarivo in an old truck with a siren. We passed our neighborhood and his school. I saw a friend in her car waiting out the traffic caused by our makeshift ambulance. She looked confused but resigned. That's often all you can be in Antananarivo. At the airport we boarded a tiny air ambulance on a three-hour flight to Pretoria.

When they arrived, everything had been set up for them. Sam still remembers the excitement and almost-fun ambulance ride to the Little Company of Mary Hospital. There was a family room where Jodi could shower and brush her teeth after two straight days of running around. The sleeper chair next to her child's bed felt almost luxurious after the previous 24 hours of makeshift medical care. At this point she finally started to have a sense that they were going to be okay.

Diabetes education and training for both began as soon as they were settled. Sam was learning how to use his insulin pen independently (though this was later nixed by the American medical team), while Jodi learned more about the illness itself and how to count and control carbohydrates. Sam seemed to have no fear, but Jodi felt overwhelmed. "I thought, 'I will never, ever know this stuff,' but now I can look at someone's plate and calculate the carbs like it's nothing," she says nonchalantly.

"He was so earnest and stoic," Jodi says of her little boy. She would have to leave him alone in his hospital room for an hour in the morning and an hour in the afternoon for training. She worried about leaving him, but when it was time for her to go, he'd say, "Okay, Mommy, I'm fine." He'd color and watch movies. "He's like a duck," she says. "Things roll off him."

She explained to him what was happening to his body and why he needed the medicine through the needle. He asked her if it would be "forever" and cried just a little bit after she said, "Yes, forever — It's like if you have to wear glasses. Everyone's body is different," she explained.

Fortunately, again, they had good friends in Pretoria who visited during the down times and brought toys for Sam. After a few days, they were discharged to a nearby hotel and continued with outpatient monitoring for week. Jodi created a daily routine for them; they visited the zoo and joined another family for a safari, and she continued with her meditation and coaching course work. "The fear of not being able to function made me commit to structure," she says. Nights were harder. Without the monitors and medical staff backing her up, she awoke every hour to check that Sam was breathing.

Sam remembers that time like it was so much fun. "That's when we had our South Africa adventure!" he says when he sees pictures from those days. I don't look back on those days negatively. It reinforced why I went into coaching. It's not necessary to live disconnected from your experience.

Whatever it takes to learn how to be with what's

happening, that's where it is. Whatever your role is, whether as a coach or a parent, when you can help people be close to, and understand, what they're experiencing, that's how we learn. That's the process of life.

Before the week was up, Jeremy and the other children joined them in Pretoria. Arrangements had been made for them to see a pediatric endocrinologist at Dell Children's Hospital in Austin, Texas, where Jodi's folks lived.

Jodi called the endocrinologist as soon as they landed, thinking they'd make an appointment in the coming days. "He'll need to be admitted today," said the doctor. This was the third country and hospital admission in less than two weeks. "Do I have time for a shower?" Jodi asked.

Shower time granted, and kids settled with grandparents, Jeremy, Jodi, and Sam headed to the hospital for a 24-hour observation. Culturally, there were some differences in practice and re-training that had to happen (like the measurement system and disposing of needles after every use instead of at the end of every day).

Jeremy was able to stay for several weeks before heading back to Madagascar, giving them all time to reconnect and for himself and Jodi to process the shift that was happening in their lives as parents. She and the kids stayed with her parents for six months before the whole family relocated to Washington D.C., together.

Jodi describes this phase of the transition as stabilizing and grounding for them all. They had access to high-quality diabetes support and services. The boys got to attend Camp

Bluebonnet together, a summer camp for families affected by diabetes. They all spent time with dear family members in ways they'd never been able to before.

There are hidden gifts in tribulation. "It's something that strips you down and connects you to your core self, whatever that may be ... love, compassion, gratitude. I let my emotions be there," says Jodi, "and now, I know I can do hard things." She also acknowledges the important role that her meditation and mindfulness practice played in keeping the "overwhelm" at bay, allowing her to support Sam in a way that helped him to thrive under duress.

The overarching gift in their experience as a family has been friendship, she explains.

"People may think that expats can't build close friendships, but that's not true at all." To others living a mobile lifestyle, she stresses, "Do not discount the relationships you build with people. That saved us — not just the things people did, but the love people showed us."

There are so many lessons we've learned — about health, gratitude, love, friendship, family — but only now am I realizing that what mattered most was simply that we kept breathing.

How blessed I am now to have seen what it's like to really breathe, to be so fully absorbed in the in and out of breath as to know that it is the most important thing. Not how you do it, for how long or for why, but simply that you breathe. And when you need it most, the rest will fall away and you'll have the in and out.

Sometimes you'll find it may be all you really need.

Carolyn Parse Rizzo, of Interval Coaching & Consulting, helps global families thrive through health and vitality challenges and change by offering individual life coaching, free resources, and child life consultation. She is a Certified Professional Coach (ACC), Certified Child Life Specialist, gentle yoga instructor, mom to a cross-cultural kid, and sweetie to an Italian neurosurgeon. Carolyn has been featured on The Mindful Expat and The Expat Happy Hour podcasts and has presented on stress and coping at the Johns Hopkins Children's Center in Baltimore, Maryland, l'Ospedale pediatrica Bambino Gesù di Roma, and Army Community Services at the United States Army Garrison-Vicenza in Italy.

Jodi Harris is a mother of three, wife of a U.S. diplomat, certified coach (ACC), trained clinical social worker, Personal Leadership facilitator, mindfulness teacher, and writer. She has over 15 years experience working with individuals outside of their home cultures and offers one-on-one coaching, group coaching, and facilitation through her company World Tree Coaching LLC.

A "Stubborn Survivor" of Parkinson's Disease

By Paul Rohrlich

My wife and I moved to Canada in 1998 with our two toddlers. It was a stressful relocation from the tropical breezes and sun of Haiti to the arctic winds of Ottawa. Between the moves in and out of temporary housing, it took quite a while to get settled and get used to our new home.

In late 1999 and early 2000, I began to notice a twitch in my left hand. I also experienced painful leg cramps that woke me at night. These symptoms began to interfere with my writing (I'm left-handed) and my sleep. I had always been the picture of good health — active, athletic, clean eating and a non-smoker — so I wasn't initially alarmed. I chalked these problems up to the tension and fatigue that accompanied a move to a new position, a new house and new country, all while raising two extremely energetic boys. But as the involuntary movements became more pronounced, I finally raised it with my doctors and, throughout 2000, went through a battery of evaluations and tests.

In early 2001, I learned the results. That gray, bleak

February day, typical of winter in Ottawa, seemed a fitting setting for the doctor's equally bleak verdict. My twitching left thumb and muscle cramps were likely multiple sclerosis (MS), he said, and I would need more tests. He had done a CAT scan, X-rays and a variety of other tests to rule out amyotrophic lateral sclerosis (ALS) and brain tumors, but this diagnosis still left me shell-shocked. I couldn't quite believe it.

Eventually, he ruled out MS and declared definitively that I suffered from early-onset Parkinson's disease (PD). I knew about Parkinson's: it was an old people's disease, one that affected my Great-Aunt Esther, whose handwriting got shakier with each passing birthday card. But I was only 44 years old, with a young family (my wife, two sons ages 4 and 5), a promising career that I truly enjoyed and lots to look forward to in life. I asked him to double-check that he had the right lab report.

Aside from the initial trauma on receiving this news, my wife and I realized we didn't really know much about this disease. And whether and when to tell others about my diagnosis was an immediate concern. As a Foreign Service Officer (FSO) for the U.S. Department of State, I had served in Zaire (now the Democratic Republic of the Congo), Japan, Madagascar and Haiti. With 14 years of service completed and intending to serve again in hardship posts overseas — which was required to move up the ladder in the State Department — I knew that having my medical clearance withdrawn would be a kiss of death to Foreign Service advancement. An officer commits to worldwide availability (i.e., implicit good health).

Being the perpetual optimist, I told myself that this couldn't be the first time that a disability struck the FSO corps, and

114

there must be some way to continue doing the fascinating job that I loved. But I soon found that I was pretty much on my own. The State Department medical department had few resources to offer. Parkinson's was a medical disqualification that was rarely — if ever — found among the people the State Department recruited. If it did strike my colleagues, they likely kept it under wraps for career-promotion reasons, if they weren't already retired.

On My Own: Opting for Optimism

I started furtively researching Parkinson's. Thankfully, the internet made information more accessible, Ottawa had excellent libraries, and I lived close enough to the United States to avail myself of American resources such as the Parkinson's Foundation and its voluminous website.

The more I read about Parkinson's (and given my lack of family history of the disease), the more it appeared that my diagnosis may have been triggered by my Foreign Service work and residence. As an economic and environment reporting officer, I had been frequently trudging through farmers' fields, investigating rumored toxic waste areas, or visiting developing world factories with few Occupational Safety and Health Administration worker health standards. I had served in severely underdeveloped places like Congo, Madagascar and Haiti. I recall that during this time, some of my colleagues became ill from exposure to chemical fumigations in their government housing.

While in Madagascar, for example, our house was infested with bedbugs and had fleas in the parquet floors. The State Department response was to fumigate the aging mattresses three times in a few short months: probably not advisable for our health, given the products available. Exposure to noxious fertilizers, chemicals and poor environmental conditions are now thought to be elements that may trigger Parkinson's, particularly if one has a genetic make-up that predisposes one to the disease.

Hanging on to a quote by a 19th-century British essayist that "History is not what happens to a man, but what he does with what happens to him," I decided to treat my disease as a manageable chronic illness, not unlike diabetes, which affects many persons, regardless of profession or age. Indeed, I would use Parkinson's to prove the point that the United States should be represented overseas not just by people of many different ethnicities and races, but by persons with great capabilities beyond their disabilities, limps and even shakes! America's diverse society should be its trademark abroad, representing its strength through its diversity. New medications and treatments were coming on stream that made living with PD possible, a better option than just succumbing to physical decline.

At times my optimism was met with a stark realism in the competitive world of diplomacy, however. Some disabilities were clearly more acceptable than others, and I soon discovered that some of my old-school colleagues were less than supportive; their comments about others with medical issues prompted me to avoid disclosing my diagnosis for several years. Some of them made clear they would step over colleagues in their pursuit of promotion up the ladder.

Managing the Illness

At the same time, my wife and I planned for the future. We needed to transition her back into the workforce to eventually take over support of the family while I continued to work for as long as possible. I put myself on a rigorous routine of exercise and diet to maintain my ability to function in "able-bodied" society. This was a daily battle. I started doing strength and stretching exercises when getting up each morning to counteract the muscles and tendons that seem to tighten up overnight. At the time, my left foot was just beginning to drag a bit, but I could still run and ski, and Canada was a beautiful place to get out and exercise! I walked as much as I could — at least a mile every morning and a mile in the late afternoon or evening — to keep my legs strong and make walking automatic again instead of a conscious process.

After a few years of playing crypto-PD patient, I was relieved when State Department medical officials were accommodating and granted me a Class 2 medical clearance, which allowed me to continue my career and still left available to me many developed and developing countries with access to good health care.

I was posted to Belgium, where my family and I remained for the next four years. I was plagued on and off by terrible reactions to the European-sourced PD medications, which left me alternately nauseated or drowsy.

My problems with mobility and balance became more pronounced, and I had to work harder to maintain and retrain my legs each morning to avoid the tyranny of small steps that PD imposes.

Despite their charms, quaint European cobblestone streets and older mass transit systems were not disability-friendly. I routinely went to the gym — at least three times a week — to maintain strength and balance. I believe that exercise and weight training remain the most essential self-help one can practice, in addition to diet.

A devout coffee drinker, I gave up caffeine to reduce its effect on my tremors and minimize any interference with sleep. I also limited my intake of refined sugar and sodium, which was pretty challenging in the pastry-rich environment of Belgium and France. Although my wife and I had always been mindful about maintaining a healthy family diet, a lower protein regime eating less red meat and more fruits and vegetables proved necessary and helpful. There is no doubt that this type of diet relieves some of PD's nonmotor symptoms.

These years of trying to balance my Parkinson's with a hectic work schedule continued when I took on a final four-year assignment in Tel Aviv, followed by shorter assignments in Paris and Reykjavík. In all, I was able to continue working for another 15 years after my initial diagnosis, taking up diplomatic responsibilities in some of our most active posts.

Fortunately, I had the Americans with Disabilities Act (ADA) behind me to facilitate "reasonable accommodation" in the workplace, when I needed items such as ergonomic keyboards and better desk chairs. Desks that permit standing and good chairs when sitting are essential for people with Parkinson's. For persons working in the U.S. public and private sectors, the ADA provides support and protection to those who continue to operate in the mainstream workplace. However, working in international environments has distinct challenges in that management does not always ensure reasonable accommodations.

Fortunately, when I opted for early retirement a few years ago at 58, I found the Parkinson's Foundation was the ideal group through which to channel my energies and practice my economic and science officer skills. Through its online resources and references I researched PD and the drugs and treatments for it thoroughly. I enrolled in a number of clinical studies, trained with the foundation to become a patient advocate and became an activist for furthering PD research, lobbying Congress to increase funding for training and boosting awareness of the growing numbers of patients, soon to reach one million Americans. Ultimately, I had the good fortune to join the foundation's People with Parkinson's Advisory Council, where we try to guide the agenda we pursue as the voice of the PD patient and caretaker community.

Although my sons may have never known their father without a limp or a "shaky" left hand, as they used to say, PD has not kept us from traveling and enjoying many experiences and outdoor activities together as a family, just as we did before my diagnosis — albeit with some modifications and more preplanning.

It has been 18 years since that bleak day in Ottawa, and I still try to maintain the structure and discipline of my working life. I wake up and practice a stretching-cum-yoga routine every morning. I have an agenda of support groups I assist and PD clinical research in which I participate. Of course, there are also many medical appointments to keep. And exercise remains the foundation of my PD management program.

I have come to a standoff with the disease: Parkinson's may in part define what I am — a stubborn 18-year survivor — but it does not define who I am. Despite having achieved a small personal success, I often think about how the State Department manages employees with long-term medical challenges — or fails to do so. With the aging population of the United States, more people are working years longer to save for retirement. The incidence of chronic illnesses such as heart disease, diabetes, lupus, Parkinson's, MS and others is increasing, particularly as the workforce ages.

If we have confidence that America's ethnic and racial diversity represents us boldly abroad, what about persons with handicaps, limited mobility or those managing medical challenges? Clearly, outstanding professional competence must be the paramount consideration; but to ignore the capabilities of those who want to serve and have the capacity to contribute is unfair to the candidate and shortchanges the department.

Paul Rohrlich is a retired State Department FSO whose recent posts include Paris, Reykjavík and Tel Aviv, where he was the environment, science, technology and health counselor. During 28 years in the Foreign Service, he also served in Kinshasa, Tokyo, Antananarivo, Port-au-Prince, Ottawa and Brussels. In Washington, D.C., he served in the Office of Development Finance. He has authored several academic articles and co-authored the book Peace and Disputed Sovereignty *(University Press of America, 2002). He is married to Susan Sandler, who is the deputy U.S. special envoy for Holocaust issues, and has two children.*

Getting Schooled in South Africa

By Sarah Showell

"Are you Jewish?" asked the school counselor.

My anxiety surged. "No," I said.

"Then why do you want to send your child to a Jewish school?" This woman was grilling us like a prosecuting attorney, and I shrank into my chair.

The principal at this Herzlia campus had welcomed us into the room and apologized that he and his colleague were running late. "We had to tell a family that their child with special needs wasn't a good fit for our school anymore, and as you can imagine, they had a lot of questions," he explained.

I should have known then that the meeting didn't bode well for us. This campus wasn't eager to enroll another disabled child, which surprised my husband and me, because we thought this meeting was a formality: all we had to do was meet the principal and sign the enrollment papers.

When my husband's company relocated our family from Lusaka, Zambia, to Cape Town, South Africa, we knew we'd upgraded to a first-class city: artisanal restaurants, stunning hikes, and first-rate health care. Our two older children made a smooth transition to the French school, and we were now searching for a welcoming school for our youngest child, Oliver, who has Down syndrome. In Zambia, Oliver had thrived at a Montessori preschool with neurotypical peers, and we wanted him to continue in a mainstream classroom. Several people recommended Herzlia Schools, the Jewish school system, because they integrated children with disabilities into their classrooms.

Oliver and I first visited the Herzlia Constantia primary campus. We had heard that this particular school loved and welcomed several children with Down syndrome, and we were able to see it firsthand. Typical second graders greeted Oliver like he was a normal kid, because they had been exposed to other children with disabilities. While there was no room for Oliver at that location, the staff there was sure that their campus in our neighborhood would welcome Oliver. Unfortunately, that was not the case.

The principal said, "I know you've probably heard this from other schools as an excuse, but we really don't have room for Oliver at our school."

Indeed, I had heard the "Sorry, we're full" line about two dozen times. One school, despite having notices posted around my neighborhood recruiting new students, told me they weren't accepting new students. Another school said that their waiting list had kids on it who were still *in utero*.

The most outrageous excuse, however, came from a public school which said they couldn't accommodate Oliver because they didn't have a wheelchair ramp. A wheelchair ramp? My kid was intellectually delayed, but he could walk. He had climbed Table Mountain — a 700-meter elevation gain in a three-kilometer hike! Despite these setbacks, I had remained optimistic that Herzlia would come through for me.

What were we doing in Africa? While my husband was transferred to Africa to work with an NGO helping children access education, our own child wasn't able to go to school. If we were back home in Seattle, Oliver would be going to an excellent public school in our neighborhood. By living in Cape Town, was I sacrificing my own child's future?

I'd been stoic with the rejections from other schools, but something broke when the principal said there was no space for Oliver. "I feel like my child is a monster and schools are scared of him," I said. "Everybody is nice about it, but they all say no. I don't have any more options." I wiped the tears from my eyes and composed myself.

The principal's face softened and he asked his colleague, "What about Cheryl in Sea Point? She might have space."

He picked up the phone and scheduled an appointment for us. Two days later, Cheryl, the director of the Herzlia Sea Point campus, welcomed us into her office, introduced us to her special needs coordinator, Elaine, and asked us to describe Oliver. I handed her Oliver's IEP and four years of school records from the Montessori school in Zambia.

She thumbed through the paperwork and nodded her head. "Well, we've never had a child with Down syndrome at this school," she said.

Oh great, I thought. Here comes the bad news...

"But we've always wanted one!" Cheryl said, clapping her hands together. I looked at her, wondering if I'd misunderstood. "Are you saying yes?" I confirmed.

"Yes! We'd love to have him, although ..." she said somberly, "we cannot guarantee that he'll have a spot later in Grade 1 for elementary school."

"Oh, that's okay!" I said. Then I cried again. This time from joy.

We left the school with a letter of acceptance. We now had six weeks to hire a facilitator to work with Oliver in the classroom and apply for a study visa for Oliver from the South African government.

We gathered certified copies of his unabridged birth certificate and current passport, our marriage certificate and passports, letters from ourselves and the school in support of his application, a utility bill confirming our South African residence, proof of medical insurance, three months of original stamped bank statements, power of attorney forms, and a medical certificate form. The medical form was our biggest concern, because the doctor had to declare if Oliver was "mentally disordered in any way, including all forms of mental retardation." I worried that the South African government would deny a study visa for Oliver since my friend had her family's visa application denied in New Zealand because her son had Down syndrome.

We submitted our comprehensive stack of documents to immigration and waited for their verdict. Cheryl and I interviewed candidates to be Oliver's classroom facilitator. This person, hired by the school, but funded by our family, was to assist him in the classroom.

The visa came through in time, and Oliver started kindergarten in January with Callyn, the facilitator-extraordinaire, by his side. On the second day of school, a couple of children met Oliver and mocked his speech. Cheryl knew that these children were just making sense of their world and she promptly met with all three kindergarten classes. She read a book called My Friend Has Down Syndrome, and the dialogue began. Children were invited to ask questions about Oliver but were banned from teasing him. Cheryl sent out an email to the parents describing what had happened and asking the parents to continue the conversation with their children. She also encouraged parents to talk to me if they had any further questions about Down syndrome.

One mom asked her daughter if she noticed anything different about Oliver. The girl said, "Yes. He has a lot of freckles."

This made me smile, but I was afraid that the kids might at best tolerate Oliver and, at worst, exclude him. I appreciated that he'd be given the opportunity to go to school, but I feared it wouldn't be long before it all fell apart. Happily, it never did. His class embraced him, and the staff went out of their way to help him.

Not long after Oliver started at his new school, Cheryl asked me to speak at a PTA fundraiser about our journey with

Oliver. I started from the beginning: I shared the fact that we were determined to adopt, and my feelings of embarrassment and guilt at getting pregnant unexpectedly. I talked about how sick I was, vomiting several times a day for the entire pregnancy. I spoke of being heartbroken for the baby girl in Ethiopia that we'd planned to adopt. We'd spent so much time and money on preparing our dossier for the adoption agency, and now that dream was tabled due to the unexpected pregnancy. I told them of the shame I felt when my friends struggling with infertility learned that we'd conceived accidentally.

I revealed what it's like to be told at birth that your child had Down syndrome, a hole in his heart, and was failing to thrive for months after he was born. I spoke of falling madly in love with Oliver and seeing his personality over his disability. He was an ideal baby: cuddly, cute, and serene. I loved this baby just as much as my other children, and he was a perfect fit for our family. After my speech, women from the school disclosed their own parenting struggles and concerns. Eight months after moving to Cape Town, I was finally connecting with others.

Prior to our move to Cape Town, we had lived in Zambia and hosted weekly dinner parties at our home. Being an expatriate there had its challenges: power cuts, dysfunctional bureaucracies, limited entertainment options, and homesickness. The antidote was sharing a meal with friends, occasionally by candlelight. Most of our friends worked in community development and could relate to the idiosyncrasies of this lifestyle.

We loved our life in Zambia, but in Cape Town we had struggled to find friends, until Oliver joined the Jewish school, where community is a priority. Almost immediately, his friends invited him to their birthday parties and playdates. He was more popular than the rest of his family members combined. I was thrilled that he had so much going on, but managing his social schedule began to wear on me a bit, and by the end of the second term I was really ready for our family vacation to Thailand during the monsoon season. We took planes, trains, boats and tuk-tuks up and down the country. We saw Asian elephants, Buddhist temples and remote islands.

One stop was a ziplining tour through the jungle. After we had signed release forms and paid for the experience, the receptionist told us that Oliver couldn't go on the adventure.

"Why not?" I asked.

She stammered. "Well, he is not well."

I smiled, knowing she was referring to his extra chromosome. "What do you mean? He's totally fine," I said checking his forehead for a fever.

"Does he have Down syndrome?" she asked.

"Yes."

"Then he cannot go, because he is disabled."

I imagined trying to explain this to Oliver. "Oliver, you can't go zip lining, because this woman decided you aren't capable."

If Oliver had any idea that they weren't going to let him go due to his disability, he would have been furious. Luckily, my husband convinced the guides to take him tandem. About halfway through the tour, Oliver turned to the guides and said, "MYSELF!" He wanted to do the zipline alone like the rest of us. The guides agreed, and my "disabled" kid tore through the jungle like a spider monkey. I made sure to tell the receptionist how amazing my kid was — and the guides backed me up.

I wish we could have stayed in Thailand longer, but reality summoned us home. Oliver needed to apply for first grade at the elementary school, the spot that Cheryl had told us she couldn't guarantee during our initial interview. The procedure involved an application and a meeting with the principal of the elementary school.

After some small talk about Oliver, the principal remarked "Well, we've never had a child with Down syndrome in our school."

I waited for him to say, "And we don't have the resources to meet his needs."

Anton continued, "... so this is a very new experience for us."

I read his face for clues. He was concerned about the challenges Oliver posed. I held my breath.

"We are open to giving it a shot and evaluating as we go."

It was a yes!

I wanted to assure him and say, "Don't worry, I had never had a child with Down syndrome until Oliver came. We are all about winging it too and evaluating it as we go."

We thanked Anton for giving Oliver a slot. Before we left his office, Anton added, "I have to warn you however, I can't guarantee he'll get into the middle school." Eric and I smiled. We had six years until we had to deal with that.

Before first grade started, we had a meeting with ten staff from the preschool and elementary school. The teachers shared tips with each other.

"Just so you know, Oliver hates stickers, so don't use that as a reward," his kindergarten teacher said.

"He also hates candy," another teacher added. "One time I gave him a piece, and he spit it on the ground."

Then Cheryl teared up and said, "We are really going to miss Oliver. Please bring him by for visits."

The elementary school teachers told us how excited they were to have him join the school.

Fast forward a few months, and Oliver is now finishing the first term of first grade. His teacher Haidee, the support teacher Renee, and his classroom aide Callyn are pushing him to work hard. They don't tolerate his ornery antics, and he adores them. Sometimes, however, Oliver can really put his foot down. I saw this in action on Sports Day a few weeks ago.

As an American, I have trouble comprehending how important Sports Day is to South Africans. The Jewish South Africans have taken the obsession to a whole new level by assigning kids to one of three teams: Maccabees, Gideon, and Samson. If your parent was on Team Gideon twenty years ago, then you are automatically are on Team Gideon, unless your other parent was, say, on Team Samson. Then your parents will need to battle this one out.

Oliver got assigned to Team Maccabees, and all I knew was we needed to wear red for Sports Day, and that "Maccabees" is pronounced Ma-KAH-beez in this country. The cheers, chants and competition at Sports Day were spectacular. In fact, Oliver was overwhelmed with the level of enthusiasm, and he didn't want to participate.

All of his teachers tried to help, but Oliver wouldn't budge. They called me over to see if I could do anything. Even Oliver's big brother Isaac gave it a shot.

Finally, I grabbed Oliver's hand and we walked to the starting line to watch the kids line up and run the race. I pleaded. I begged. I bribed him with ice cream. After everyone finished this race and moved to a different part of the field, I decided Oliver, his brother, and I would jog the racecourse. I figured the spectators would be focused on the other events, so Oliver wouldn't feel any pressure.

Oliver still refused to stand up, so I threatened him with the most drastic punishment I could imagine. He popped up, grabbed my hand on one side and Isaac's on the other, and we jogged the racecourse. I prayed no one would notice us, but everyone saw our catawampus race and cheered for Oliver. Turns out the child who hates stickers and candy will do anything for applause. He picked up his pace and finished the impromptu race.

A teacher later confided, "I hate doing this event every year, because some parents are all about the winning and miss the whole point. Oliver just redeemed the day for me."

After running with his brother and me, Oliver eagerly participated in the other races. Kids, even those from the other teams, cheered him on. After one race, his good friend Ari came up to us and said, "You know, Oliver's relay team came in last place."

I smiled. There's always that one kid who needs to report the obvious.

Then he grinned, "Just like me! My relay team was in last place too!"

I gave Ari a high five for being so awesome. He and Oliver were both on Team Maccabees, which didn't win this year's Sports Day competition. I'm not worried though. We still have six more years of Sports Days ahead of us and, depending on whether Oliver gets a spot in the middle school, we may have an additional six years. Meanwhile I'll savor this time when life has come together. The world is kinder to Oliver than I could ever have thought.

Sarah Showell is an author writing her first young adult novel about sex trafficking. For fun she loves making all sorts of art, watching stand-up comedy, and guessing which country her Uber driver is from. Sarah lives with her husband, three children, and chocolate Labrador in Cape Town.

If in Doubt, Evacuate Right Away; and Don't Drink the Water

By Lior Ben-Ami

It all started on a beautiful Monday, November 8, 1999, in the quiet Cocody neighborhood in Abidjan, Côte d'Ivoire. Early in the morning, I took our newly adopted puppy for a walk. Everything seemed fine — the beginning of another week in our West African adventure.

Fourteen months earlier, I had accompanied my wife, Nina — an Israeli diplomat — to her posting as the embassy's deputy chief of mission in Côte d'Ivoire. We fell in love with Africa soon after arriving: the people, culture, gorgeous sandy beaches, lush and wild green landscapes, food, music, colorful markets … Abidjan was very safe and vibrant at the time.

But on that Monday, my African honeymoon ended abruptly. After walking the dog, Nina and I drove to the embassy where I worked as a regional IT manager, covering technology needs for Israel's embassies throughout West

Africa. After about two hours, something felt wrong. It suddenly seemed hard for me to get up from my chair and my fingers felt slow when I typed. It was a very strange feeling. I thought I must just be very tired from the deep-sea fishing we had done the day before. My legs got weaker and weaker. I felt as if I had heavy weights on them. I told Nina and she agreed it must be tiredness. "You should go to sleep early tonight," she said, "and everything will get back to normal."

However, by the time I came home, I couldn't even climb the stairs; Nina had to drag me. Because we had heard so much about the medical hazards of West Africa, I was afraid I had contracted a deadly strain of malaria, or maybe Ebola, or a nasty streptococcal infection. I joked that Nina would have to work hard sending my coffin back to Israel. "Just think of all the paperwork," I said, trying to find the humor. "I'm so sorry you'll have to go through all of this bureaucracy." But Nina didn't laugh. She became more and more worried and far less convinced that all I needed was a good night's sleep.

At home, we quickly decided to visit the local hospital. Fortunately, going down the stairs was a bit easier than going up; I could sit and slide down. To say the hospital was modestly equipped would be an understatement. It was around 7 p.m., and most of the staff was gone. The remaining nurses didn't know what to do with me other than take my blood pressure and check my temperature. I needed to go to the toilet and Nina helped me in, but afterwards, I couldn't get up and two male nurses had to lift me. It was humiliating. Little did I know that my very near future would bring more of these types of incidents.

"You can sleep here or come back tomorrow to see a doctor,"

a nurse told me. I had always hated hospitals and since I had no access to a doctor, I chose to head back home to get some sleep and return again in the morning. Deep down inside I was holding onto that fantasy that all I needed was a good sleep and I would wake up from a bad dream.

We went back home. The mighty stairs again. Once safely inside, I sat on an office chair with wheels, so I could move around. I could see the growing worry on Nina's face. She called her uncle, a doctor. We tried surfing the web, searching for terms like "weak legs" and "sudden body weakness," but found no real answers. Falling asleep was challenging to say the least, but eventually we both did.

I woke early because I had to go to the bathroom. But I couldn't.

I literally could not move. At all. Not even a finger. Nothing. It was bizarre. I was lying in bed, on my back, feeling completely normal, feeling my arms and legs like it was just another lazy morning, but when I tried to move, nothing happened. I was stuck. "I'm doomed," I thought to myself. "This is it. It's only a matter of hours." I woke Nina by calling her name frantically to tell her what was going on. She called an ambulance.

We made it back to the same hospital, now with doctors. I was put in a wheelchair, asked a bunch of questions and then taken for an EMG test. It was nice to learn that this modestly equipped hospital had a new, state of the art EMG machine courtesy of the Canadian government. I had no idea what an EMG test was. The very nice, friendly Ivorian neurologist, who had studied medicine in France explained the basics: the test checks muscle responses and nerve conductivity. A little painful, but not too bad.

"It looks like Guillain-Barré syndrome," said the neurologist after carefully looking at the EMG results for ten very long minutes. "In order to be completely sure, a lumbar puncture must be performed, but we can't do it here, and we can't treat you here. You should leave Côte d'Ivoire as soon as possible. By the way, were you sick in the last week? A flu? Fever? Upset stomach?"

I had been sick. A few days before it all started, I had recovered from a terrible stomach flu that lasted almost a week. And I knew exactly why I'd had it.

A week and a half earlier, Nina and I had joined Mondo, a friendly expert beekeeper who was sent to Côte d'Ivoire by Israel's Ministry of Foreign Affairs to help teach local farmers how to produce honey. Mondo was working for MASHAV, Israel's Agency for International Development Cooperation, and spent his time traveling to the most deserted areas of the country to teach farmers in small, remote villages. Our destination that day was near the city of Korhogo, about a seven-hour drive north of Abidjan. We stopped at a few villages on the way and witnessed stunning art — tapestry, wooden statues and metal artifacts — all made with extremely primitive tools and means.

After many unpaved roads, we finally arrived at the village entrance, guarded by a man with a very long antique rifle decorated with engravings. Before we understood what was going on, the man shot into the air, announcing the arrival of the Israeli bee expert. We were stunned, but Mondo seemed amused. In seconds, Mondo's car was surrounded by people: men, women and children, all smiling, singing and welcoming us. We arrived at the center of the small village, which contained several mud and straw huts and one small cement cabin. We sat under a huge mango tree. There, the village chief gave a speech in the local dialect that was translated to French by one of his assistants. He thanked the State of Israel for all the help and support. And then the artistic part began: men and women played local musical instruments and started to dance, asking us to join. What a party! A man came with a small goat and offered to slaughter it on our behalf. We politely declined, explaining that according to our religion, only our chief can approve something like that (it was too complicated to explain what kosher rules or a rabbi were). They understood and offered us nuts and roots, which we accepted. They were so grateful.

And then they offered us water. Now, as one might know, water is not safe to drink in Côte d'Ivoire. During the previous 14 months, we had only consumed bottled mineral water. We didn't drink tap water in our homes or anywhere else. And now we were in a village with no electricity or running water. We knew that the water was from a local well. But we didn't want to offend our gracious hosts. We'll only take a small sip, we decided. What can happen? Worst case scenario, we naïvely thought, is that we would have an upset stomach for a day or two. Who could have imagined that a small sip of water would render me completely paralyzed from the neck down?

"The most dangerous part of Guillain-Barré syndrome is that it can affect the lungs," said the neurologist. "A small

137

percentage of people with the syndrome can suffocate and die." She made me blow into a tube and the results showed that my lungs were already affected: my lung capacity was reduced by 50%. "You can't fly in a commercial plane without a doctor or a respirator," she said. When I heard that my lungs were affected, I realized that the danger was not just to my mobility, but also to my life. How lucky I was to be in a hospital in Abidjan, with respirators if needed.

Nina kept our embassy updated and consulted with the Foreign Ministry doctor in Israel. Since there are no direct flights between Côte d'Ivoire and Israel, a doctor with a respirator travelled from Geneva to Abidjan to transport me to Switzerland. In retrospect, this was a mistake. An airborne ambulance would have been a smarter choice. Unfortunately, this option was not presented to us, and we didn't know the option existed until the doctors in Geneva mentioned it. The three days I had to wait before receiving treatment made my situation significantly worse. Guillain-Barré Syndrome (GBS for short) destroys the protective covering of the peripheral nerves — the myelin sheath — greatly reducing communication between neurons. While the myelin can slowly grow back, if the condition is not treated quickly, GBS can also affect the nerves themselves, which is irreversible. But, of course, I didn't know any of this at the time.

A mere three days after first experiencing the weakness in my legs, I arrived at the Abidjan airport, with Nina, a doctor with a respirator and the entire embassy staff who came to say goodbye. Three men from the embassy carried me on a stretcher to a bed on the commercial plane. Nina and I landed in Geneva and were taken to La Tour Hospital.

Once in Geneva, a spinal tap confirmed my GBS diagnosis, which then led to an intravenous immunoglobulin (IVIG) infusion to try to stop and reverse nerve deterioration. Armed with medical certainty, Nina wanted to inform our family in Israel and the U.S., but I didn't want to alarm my parents. I could only imagine how they would feel if they heard their son was paralyzed from the neck down. I asked Nina to tell them I had some weakness in my legs and that we were flown to a modern hospital in Geneva, but my mother decided to come right away from Israel. Nina told her parents the whole truth, and they decided that her father would fly from Washington to Geneva to support us as well.

In the hospital, I remained a prisoner of my own body. I could feel every inch of my body but couldn't move anything below my neck. I had muscle pain in my legs, back, and shoulders. I soon realized that we make tiny imperceptible movements each night as we sleep. These movements are not important until you cannot do them on your own — and then, your body can ache and become numb. Every morning, as Nina came to my room, I would ask her to scratch my cheek, "before I go crazy." Soon enough I had to swallow my pride and ask the staff for help when I needed it.

The Israeli mission to the UN in Geneva helped us feel at home. The ambassador and other diplomats at the mission who didn't actually know us came to visit a few times, to offer support. This lifted our spirits and brought some distraction from the medical emergency that had engulfed us.

Two days after I started receiving the IVIG infusion, I could move my right-hand index finger. Well, "move" was perhaps overstated. It was almost impossible to notice but I was optimistic; surely, I thought, this nightmare is starting to reverse. This coincided with the day our parents arrived, and while Nina and I were happy about the recent development about my finger, my mother was simply shocked. When she saw me, her face turned white and she started to cry. I will never forget her expression. We filled her in on the entire story and the promising prognosis, but this seemed to only help a little. However, the presence of our parents was a huge support for Nina and me. We embraced having them there and being able to share our worries. Nina's father was a rock of support, and she was able to cry on his shoulder and share the burden of this medical disaster with him, as he offered her love and some peace of mind.

Day by day, I started to move more fingers, but I still felt like a turtle stuck on its back. My hands were still very weak, and I couldn't move my arms and legs, but every little improvement made me more optimistic. Within a week or so, I was transported by a patient lift to a wheelchair. It was great to finally leave the bed. My limbs were moved by physical therapists, like a rag doll, to prevent muscle degeneration. I was also tied to a tilt bed, to maintain blood circulation. The first time, when the bed started to tilt, my body was instantly covered with cold sweat and I almost fainted. The blood pressure machine I was connected to beeped uncontrollably. But gradually, things got better.

About three weeks after arriving in Geneva, a physician from Israel came to escort me to my new home for the next nine months: the neurological rehab center, part of the Sheba hospital in Israel. It was wonderful to come home and to be surrounded by family and friends who gave me a much-needed boost of strength. After more tests and evaluations, I started a daily routine of physical and occupational therapy.

My first occupational therapy session was a big blow. I was presented with a kit with three items: a zipper, a tied shoelace, and a button with a buttonhole. I knew my hands were weak, but I didn't realize just how much. My fingers were too weak to move the zipper, untie the lace or button the button. It was extremely frustrating. A new EMG test shortly after, came as another, heavier blow. The neurologist studied the results for a long time, finally saying, "It doesn't look so good. The nerves themselves were affected, and that's irreversible. As for the myelin, the damage is significant. You are a tall guy, and myelin growth is about 1mm a day. If you ever walk again, it will take something like three years."

Here I was thinking I'm on the right track to a full recovery after having made some progress in Switzerland. I had already accepted that my recovery may take three or four months. But three years? And "if I ever walk"? Why should I even bother with all those physical therapy sessions?

I was devastated, but giving up was not an option. Almost all of my co-patients, including my roommate who became a close friend, suffered from spinal injuries. They knew they would never walk again. Still, with all those physical and mental difficulties they continued to work hard during physical therapy in order to strengthen whatever was possible. I looked up to them and told myself to work hard. After about a month, my arms got a little better and I started to slowly wheel myself around, but my fingers remained weak. I couldn't open a sugar bag at the cafeteria or light a lighter for a cigarette, but I could finally explore the hospital.

While I was confronting my limits during therapies, working

life continued for my wife. Fortunately, the Israeli Foreign Ministry was very supportive. They allowed Nina to take paid leave and stay in the hospital hotel as long as she needed, but I thought she should go back to Abidjan to continue her post. After all, I had a routine of treatments and daily visitors, as well as new hospital friends also receiving therapy, with whom I bonded over practical jokes and nightlong conversations. For Nina, our new life was much harder. She wanted to help me get better, but there was nothing she could do. For her, it was like watching grass grow. "Go back to Abidjan, and when you return for a visit, in three months or so, I'll be better," I told her. And so she went back to Abidjan.

Our life took yet again another turn when civil war broke out in Côte d'Ivoire. The peaceful country we once loved started to burn. While diplomatic family members were flown back to their home countries, Nina was instructed to stay and not leave the apartment after work. Electricity became limited and the phone landlines stopped working. One night, in poor judgment, Nina decided to go outside and call me from a public pay phone. She was lonely, she missed me and wanted to chat. It felt like we were two characters in a movie that critics would tank for being "overly dramatic." Me in Israel, sitting in a wheelchair, a nurse holding the phone to my ear, speaking to Nina in war-torn Côte d'Ivoire with background gunshots.

Months passed. With daily physical and occupational therapy sessions and with the great help of excellent therapists, my arms and hands finally got stronger. I became more independent. I could finally turn in bed, get out of bed to my wheelchair, and eat by myself. My legs, on the other hand, refused to move, even though I trained on a standing machine with locked knees daily. There was no movement whatsoever until I started hydrotherapy in the rehab pool. Inside the pool I could move my legs a little but even nine months after arriving at the center, my legs still didn't move outside of the pool.

Meanwhile, Nina received her new posting, as the consul in the Israeli Consulate General in Montreal, Canada. On the way to our new home, Nina stopped in Israel to arrange for my release. In a bittersweet final meeting with the rehab neurologists, we were told that since there had not been significant progress in my leg strength, there was a good chance I would stay in a wheelchair for life.

We arrived in Montreal August 2000. This was the first time I had travelled as a wheelchair-bound person. The challenges were many; some we had anticipated, and others came as a surprise, such as navigating the city and leading an independent life as a disabled person. For example, the Consulate General put us in a hotel downtown, with a handicapped-accessible room. Despite this accommodation, the ramp from the street to the hotel was too steep, and on our second day I fell backwards with my chair when I tried to enter the lobby. The wheelchair handles literally saved my head and neck. The Consulate moved us to another hotel, but we found it to be exceptionally difficult to find an appropriate apartment for me. There are about six months of snow every year in Montreal, and most apartment buildings have stairs at their entrance. The apartments themselves needed to have wide enough doors and corridors and large enough bathrooms for my wheelchair. It took us more than two months to find a suitable apartment. But, after almost a year in hospitals and hotels, it was great to be finally "home" again with Nina. Back to normal. Well, almost.

I started to accept the reality that the wheelchair would stay with me for good and slowly learned I could have a satisfying, even enjoyable, life in a wheelchair. We did what we had always done before I became sick. We travelled, went out, met new people. I was working at the consulate in IT and communications after some adaptations to the office like reversing the bathroom door so it would open to the outside. I also met with a Canadian neurologist who referred me to an outpatient rehab facility, the Constance-Lethbridge Rehabilitation Centre. He asked me not to give up; maybe with time and daily work, my legs would get stronger. I didn't want to get my hopes up, but I had nothing to lose, plus I had to continue working out to prevent future deterioration.

So, I quickly fell into a new routine. In the mornings I worked at the rehab center (including hydrotherapy), and in the afternoons I worked at the consulate. Slowly, with a lot of work in the pool, wearing floaties on my legs as weights, my legs got stronger. About a year later, I could finally walk, at long last! Slowly, with a walker and two ankle braces, but I was perpendicular! In the following months, I progressed to two crutches and braces, one crutch and braces, and at the end, a cane and braces. Today, almost 20 years later, I use two braces, and in long walks, also a cane.

This is the beginning of the end of my GBS story, in which I learned a lot about patience and perspective, optimism, and as clichéd as it may sound, the strength of life and the importance of family and friends. The elements which helped push me forward included my own internal determination, a good sense of humor, loving support of friends and family, my desire to make the most of a bad situation, and my sober understanding that it could have been much worse. Most of all, Nina's unconditional love and support gave me strength and the ability to endure these difficult circumstances. My friends from the rehab center in Israel became some of my closest friends; the bonds we made there remain very strong to this day.

Some lessons learned: Don't drink unsafe water! If you don't want to insult your hosts, it's better just to pretend you're drinking. Second, if you get sick abroad, get medical help as fast as possible, make sure you have medical insurance to cover life's unexpected moments, and cherish your loved ones, even though it is hard sometimes. Also equally important: Don't give up; remain optimistic — humor can be a major asset in times of crisis.

Despite the fact that GBS is now a part of me and the paralysis persists in both of my feet, requiring me to wear ankle braces, I continue to lead a full and global life. Our first daughter was born in Montreal in 2003, and our second and third daughters were born in 2007 and 2009, in Paris. We are currently back in Israel after having spent four lovely years as diplomats in Uruguay. I do hope to go back to Africa someday and enjoy the beautiful and vibrant culture, food, and beaches that I remember from our good times in Côte d'Ivoire — but this time I'll know not to drink the water!

Lior Ben-Ami is a native of Israel and is married with three daughters. He is a computer programmer and systems manager by profession and football fan by vocation. He speaks French, Spanish, and English as well as his native Hebrew, and affirms that people do speak foreign languages better under the influence of alcohol. Lior is a current event junkie and a movie aficionado who loves traveling.

Lessons in Silence: Disability, Not Inability

By Julia Inserro

When Clair Malik speaks about the hundreds of kids she calls her children, her eyes shine with pride and her hands fly even faster as she subconsciously signs as she speaks. As I follow her out to the playground during recess, it's clear that the adoration is mutual: She's instantly surrounded by many of the 70 children who attend school at the Deaf Unit in Cairo.

A few months earlier, as an accompanying U.S. Embassy spouse, I attended an embassy-sponsored tour of the school. I was so taken with the energy of the staff and children that when Clair, the school's director, said she was looking for some office help, I quickly volunteered. I had taken American Sign Language in college, but any hope I had in reviving it was quickly dashed as I learned that the students and teachers were using Egyptian Sign Language.

As a young woman, Clair spent three years in Lebanon studying to become a sign-language teacher. She then returned to her native Cairo. "I knew what God's purpose was for me," she said. So, in 1982, with the support of the Anglican Diocese of Egypt, she opened the doors of the Deaf Unit. As its director, she has been the driving force since the beginning. She started with just four students and a teacher, and today has 70 Egyptian students, ages five through sixteen. Fifty-four of them board at the school throughout the week because their families live far away in Upper Egypt. She relies now on eight teachers, 30 household and administrative staff, and Reverend Faraj Hanna, who arrived in 2007 and has been instrumental in the growth of the associated Deaf Church and the Deaf Club.

Back on the playground, I watch as Clair addresses the children pooling around her. There's a tall boy with glasses who thrusts a sketch pad at her with obvious pride. Clair tells me with a smile that John says he doesn't like carpentry; he prefers to draw. She admires his art but tells him he still must go to carpentry class.

I take this opportunity on the playground to step back and snap some photos. However, as soon as the camera is out, the divas of the Deaf Unit converge on me, led by six-year-old Nada. Camera-shy they are not, so I do my best to make sure I get photos of everyone, especially those tugging on my sweater. Even the few who are tentative at first beam after seeing their picture in digital playback. And once the divas are let loose, it's hard to rein them in. I eventually have to stop letting everyone see their photos, just so I can continue to take some. Despite our seemingly cavernous gaps in communication — my American Sign Language is useless and my Arabic is halting at best — we are all able to understand each other. The toothy grins and little hands waving the universal sign for "I love you" pretty much say it all.

As the children head back into their classrooms, Clair gives me a behind-the-scenes look at the school's facilities. There are eight classrooms, covering grades KG1 through six. Peeking in on KG1, I see four six-year-olds sitting in their chairs, attentively watching their teacher, Ms. Hanan. This lasts only a few seconds before dear Nada spots us and with a squeal of delight charges at the door. Suddenly there are four gleeful, screaming children leaping about and posing with "I love yous" waving all around. We apologize for the interruption, and Ms. Hanan attempts to regain control, but I can see Nada keeping an eye on the doorway.

We catch the rest of the classrooms in the midst of studying history, Arabic, English, geography, science, Egyptian Sign Language and math. They also teach Arabic lip-reading and voice therapy, relying on trained speech therapists working with the kids one-on-one, with amazing results. I watch in wonder as a small eight-year-old boy sits with his teacher in front of a mirror. He mimics the shape she is making her with mouth and, in turn, tries to mimic the sound. Clair says he has partial hearing, so his progress is better than that of the others. As he pushes out a loud "E" sound, his pride is evident in his smile. We all give the universal sign for applause.

We next stop in to see Gorg teaching Ra'id and Michael some of the basic names and signs for carpentry tools in their pre-vocational class. Gorg, like many of the teachers here, is also hearing-impaired, and in addition to these pre-vocational classes, he teaches and works at the Vocational Training Center (VTC) behind the school. The VTC trains and employs over 30 Egyptian hearing-impaired adults in sewing and appliqué, carpentry and metalworking. They make blankets, wall-hangings, tablecloths, baby bibs, wooden pyramid puzzles, decorative trivets, candle holders, and lots of Christmas decorations. These skills afford them the chance to become experts in their trades and further improve their quality of life by promoting social and financial independence. The VTC has earned a reputation for quality-made goods, and in addition to all their custom-made orders, the professional crafts they produce are sold in shops and bazaars in Egypt and throughout Europe.

Clair's dreams don't stop here. In 2009, they laid the foundation stone for a new state-of-the-art VTC complex out in Six October City, on the outskirts of Cairo. The goal is to increase their outreach, enabling 100 hearing-impaired adults to train in the trades they currently offer, or in any of the new classes they plan to add, such as plumbing and electricity, car repair, barbering classes and computer repair.

The next milestone to be reached, thanks in large part to donations from the Japanese Embassy in Cairo, is to open an Audiology Clinic next to the Deaf Unit. The clinic will be able to offer low-cost hearing devices to those in need and to conduct hearing tests, primarily on children, to determine the severity of loss, and to offer early intervention, for both the child and the family.

Clair confesses that while she focuses on raising funds to get computers for the children, keeping their washing machines running, and expanding outreach and opportunities for the deaf community, the two biggest hurdles for these children to overcome are family and public misconceptions. For some of the children, their family life is not always supportive of their education or their disability. On weekends, when those kids who live at the school during the week can go home, some of them beg not to leave. "No one talks to me at home," they tell Clair. While some parents take advantage of the Egyptian sign language classes and family support the Deaf Unit offers, many do not. For those children, returning home means loneliness and isolation.

In addition to working within the families, Clair and Reverend Faraj also strive to educate the public on the causes of hearing loss and the misunderstandings surrounding it. One of the primary causes for disabilities in Egypt, including deafness, is marriage among close relatives, so they have developed educational programs to inform communities of these potential problems. In addition, to better integrate the hearing-impaired and hearing communities, they sponsor math competitions, school exchanges, summer camps, and the Deaf Club, with athletic competitions open to everyone. Through these programs and Reverend Faraj's ministry through the Deaf Church, they are working to break down many of the public's fears and misconceptions about people with disabilities.

Unknowingly, I have walked in with a misconception of my own. I assumed that a "deaf" school would be a vault of silence, broken only by the creak of doors and shuffle of feet. In actuality, there is a never-ending din. The constant chatter of children's voices surrounds you, sometimes reaching pandemonium heights (and not just when Nada sees a camera). When I learn that many of these children, whom Clair identifies with the help of other non-governmental organizations and doctors throughout Egypt, arrive at the Deaf Unit having no language skills at all, it makes the commotion all the more delightful.

As I walk through the grounds of the Deaf Unit, past the VTC with its crackling soldering irons and buzzing saws, through the kitchen where today's hot lunch is being prepared, past the bedrooms stacked with bunk beds, and along the decorated classroom halls echoing with eager, new-found voices, I am in awe of what has been accomplished with one woman's sense of purpose. It's not just the physicality of the space and actuality of the classrooms. It's Clair's reminder to everyone, daily, that disability does not mean inability. As she stands on the playground, smiling and laughing amidst a swarm of signing hands, it's clear that Clair, Reverend Faraj and the staff are succeeding beyond measure in raising self-confident, independent, proud and truly delightful children, who just happen to be hearing-impaired.

Julia Inserro is a mom of three littles, living abroad with her husband and a handful of cats. She is the author of the award-winning Nonni's Moon, *her first children's book. For more information on her future releases, follow her at www.juliainserro.com.*

My Daughter Through Joan of Arc's Eyes

By Suzanne Kamata

When my daughter Lilia was 13, we fulfilled a mutual fantasy
by taking a mother-daughter trip to Paris. The journey was
complicated by my daughter's multiple disabilities — she is
deaf, and she uses a wheelchair due to cerebral palsy.
Although I am an American, Lilia's father is Japanese. We
live in rural Japan, near my husband's family. My daughter
attended the local School for the Deaf. Due to her learning
disabilities, she wasn't on the academic track. Mostly, she
spent her days learning life skills like how to make potato
salad or carrying out tasks that would prepare her for the
menial labor that severely disabled youth typically engage in
after graduation.

For me, this trip to Paris was a chance to educate my
daughter and to share my love of France with her. As a
college student in the United States, I spent a semester in
Avignon. Later, I met and married her Japanese father in
Shikoku, where we now live. I wanted to show Lilia some of
the world's greatest works of art, since she had an aptitude
for drawing and aspired to be a manga artist. I also wanted
her to learn a bit of history, knowing that she wouldn't have

any social studies or history classes in junior and senior high school.

In the first few days of our stay, we visited famous sites such as the palace at Versailles and the Louvre Museum, which, like all public museums in France (and many in Japan), are free to individuals with disabilities. Of course we went to see the Mona Lisa. As usual, a big crowd was gathered around the cordoned-off painting. However, when the other tourists saw my daughter in her wheelchair, they immediately created a path for her. The museum docent smiled and allowed Lilia inside the ropes so that she could observe the famous painting up close while the other visitors and I remained behind. A couple of days later, at the relatively inaccessible Tomb of Napoleon, strangers helped carry Lilia's wheelchair up the steps. The people of Paris were unfailingly kind to my daughter.

By day four, Lilia and I, however, were starting to get snippy with each other. The novelty of being in Paris had worn off slightly, and once again I was urging her to wash her face, brush her teeth, and put on her shoes. My plan was to take her to see the site where Joan of Arc was burned at the stake; a bit morbid, I know, but it was history. Lilia had read a manga biography of the martyred warrior girl, so she had some context. We had a big day ahead of us, but she was sitting at the hotel room desk in her pajamas playing "World of Goo" on my tablet, which I had brought along for email and research.

"Hurry up!" I signed. "We have to get to the train station! It'll take us a long time to get to Rouen."

Lilia sighed, and reluctantly closed the window on the tablet.

Slowly, slowly, she began to change her clothes while I consulted the guidebook one last time. There are various locations associated with Joan of Arc in France — such as Domrémy-la-Pucelle, where she was born around 1412, and where she, an illiterate 12-year-old peasant girl, allegedly received heavenly visions charging her with the duty to drive the marauding English occupiers out of France. There is also Orléans, where she led an army to victory at the age of 19. One of the closest related sites, however, was Rouen, an hour and a half by train from Paris, where she was imprisoned and executed for heresy.

When we were finally dressed and out the door, we took a taxi to the bustling Gare St. Lazarre. Once inside, we gazed at our surroundings for a moment before a kind gentleman approached us and offered assistance. He was, as it turned out, an employee of SNCF, the French railroad, and he knew exactly where we needed to go. He showed us to an office at the other end of the building and told the guy at the desk that we needed help getting on and off the train. I could also buy our tickets in the office.

"How old is she?" the clerk asked. "Thirteen." "If she were 12, she would be eligible for a lower fare ..." But she was almost 14. I didn't want to lie. He hesitated for a moment, then said that he was going to charge me for one adult ticket and one child's ticket. "*Merci beaucoup!*"

We waited in the quiet office, away from the jostling commuters, until it was time to board. A couple of young women in SNCF uniforms got us settled in the accessible compartment, which was new and clean and comfortable. "Beautiful!" Lilia exclaimed. When I pointed out the wheelchair-accessible toilet, she signed, "Great!"

In Rouen, more railway workers were waiting to help us get off and into the station. The town itself was small, medieval, and charming. Our first order of business was to find some lunch. We exited the station and stepped into one of the first viable restaurants we came across — La Metropole, which was adorned with a red awning and wide windows. The tables were close together, and a tight fit with the wheelchair, but we managed. Some businessmen were speaking English at the next table. A pregnant French woman was dining alone. When I opened the menu, I read that the place had once been a favorite of Simone de Beauvoir and Jean-Paul Sartre. Simone had often waited there for Jean-Paul to finish up his classes at the local university. I'd already decided that I wouldn't drag Lilia to famous hangouts of French or expat writers, which would have had little meaning for her. Back in Japan, we'd decided together that the theme of our travels would be history and art. But I was delighted to have stumbled across a literary landmark anyhow. Although I had some issues with how Simone conducted herself in her relationship with Jean-Paul, she was an icon, and her novel *The Blood of Others*, about the French Resistance, was one of my all-time favorite books.

Lilia was momentarily impressed when I explained that one of my favorite writers had frequented the restaurant where we sat. "Do you know her?" she asked via sign language. "Is she your friend?" Lilia knew that many of my friends were writers, and she'd seen their photos on book jackets after meeting them in person, so this was not an altogether ridiculous question. "No, she lived a long time ago," I explained. Certainly, I would have liked to meet her. "She was very famous. I just read her books."

As lunch progressed, I noticed that Lilia had tomato sauce on her mouth. I pointed to the napkin, and to my own lips. She sighed gustily before wiping her own face and then threw her napkin down on the table. Once back on the sidewalk, she threw her arms down in the sign for "tired," and sat in her wheelchair, immobile. By this time, my shoulders were aching from pushing her all over Paris, yet having gone over the daily budget I had calculated for us the past two days, I was reluctant to take any more cabs. I also found her level of enthusiasm insufficient. After all, it would have been easier to hang out in Paris, maybe visit the Orsay Museum, than to schlep all the way to Normandy.

"Give me the camera," she signed. I knew that she would want to take pictures of every little thing. When we had gone to the Louvre a few days earlier, she had photographed the paintings, the ceilings, and the food we ate in the cafeteria. "Let's just look at things for now," I said. I wanted to hang on to the camera to make sure that I got some publishable photos in case I sold a travel essay on this expedition.

We followed a sign down a cobbled side street and came across the dungeon where Joan had been imprisoned during her last days. It wasn't open to tourists that day, which was just as well because I'd read that there were only stairs leading to the chamber where she was kept; it wasn't wheelchair accessible. We stood for a few minutes looking up at the grey conical tower. I tried to imagine being trapped inside without any windows, without any hope.

Most historians agree that Joan's arrest was politically motivated, and that her trial was unfair. Although she was apprehended for heresy, the charge was not considered a capital offense unless it was repeated. Historians who've studied the court transcripts have remarked upon her intelligence. She had no education, but she did great things. Although I knew that Joan was still discussed six hundred years after her birth because she was so exceptional, I couldn't help but be encouraged by her humble beginnings. My daughter might have only read at a second-grade level, but Joan couldn't read at all.

After taking a few requisite photos, we moved on. We found the Rouen Cathedral, which dates from the 11th century and figures in the background of at least one painting of Joan's death. The original spires have been struck by lightning, blown down by wind, and damaged by fire. During World War II, bombs fell upon the cathedral, and the resulting conflagration melted the bells. Although Lilia and I didn't go inside, I found out later that the heart of Richard the Lionhearted was entombed within, as well as the entire body of John Lancaster, Duke of Bedford, who is considered to be Joan of Arc's murderer.

Perhaps from paintings, I had this vague idea that Joan had been burned at the stake right in front of this cathedral. However, there were no markers or monuments to indicate the exact site. Also, there was no Joan of Arc paraphernalia in the gift shop just adjacent to the square. I realized that she must have spent her final moments somewhere else.

I bought a guide to Rouen in Japanese, to the confusion of the young man at the cash register. Clearly, I was an English-speaking American. "For my daughter," I explained, and asked where Joan had been executed. He drew me a little map.

Meanwhile, Lilia seemed more interested in window

shopping at the H&M off the square, or stopping for a snack. I was trying to find the Eglise de Jean d'Arc, while she was bugging me for a drink. "We need to find the place where she died!" I insisted. We needed to pay homage to this amazing, brave young woman. Why should we care, in this moment, about the latest fashions? I charged on.

We passed a man in a wheelchair. Lilia looked up at me as if she wanted an explanation, but I shook my head slightly, and signed that I would tell her more later. It didn't seem polite to talk about the man in front of him, even if we were using a language he didn't understand.

We went under a gilded clock, past windows full of Easter chocolate — rabbits on skis, Pingu with a fish in his mouth — and macarons in many flavors. We passed another shop with candy flower bouquets. "Look!" I pointed out an array of Hello Kitty lollipops to Lilia. She gestured to the camera. I handed it over and let her take some photos of the familiar Japanese character. And then finally we came across the Tears of Our Lady of Rouen Bakery. I figured Our Lady referred to Joan. We must be getting closer, I thought.

Finally, there it was: a simple wooden cross rising into the air. A sign declaring "Le Bucher. The location where Joan of Arc was burnt May 30th, 1431." It was humble, like Joan herself. Lilia gasped with surprise and remarked that she was born on May 30, the anniversary of the day that Joan died — a cosmic connection. We threw our heads back, looked up at the cross, and observed a moment of silence. And then, to sweeten our sorrow, we indulged in Nutella crepes.

By the time we finally entered the H&M near the cathedral, Lilia had mellowed. Instead of exclaiming over the racks of

159

cute clothes, she wheeled herself slowly through the store, her thoughts seemingly elsewhere. She was no longer in consumer mode. "I want to give some money to that man," she signed. "Okay." I handed her a coin and stood back as she wheeled herself to the guy in the wheelchair. A woman was next to him, maybe his wife. When Lilia gave him the money, they gestured to an array of ashtrays made out of recycled cans. Lilia chose one. They nodded and smiled at each other, and then Lilia waved good-bye.

On the way to the train station, where we would catch our train back to Paris, we saw another guy sitting with his back against a building, a cardboard sign at his side. This man wasn't selling anything. He looked dejected. Defeated. The sign said, "Out of work. Three kids at home."

Later, back at our hotel, I asked Lilia, "What was the most interesting thing about today?" "The train," she said. "It was my first time."

I was a bit surprised that Joan of Arc didn't have more of an impact. Or that she hadn't been more impressed by the Nutella crepes (a specialty of Normandy!), but the train was nice, observing the countryside from our plush purple seats was very peaceful.

Lilia became pensive. "There were a lot of people without money," she signed.

I nodded. Of course she was surprised to see people asking for hand-outs. No one begged in Japan. If there was poverty, it was hidden. I explained that in France people who are unemployed can go to museums for free. The French understand that art is important and everyone — those with disabilities, children, the poor — is allowed access to the Mona Lisa. "Isn't that great?"

She nodded, but she still seemed haunted by the beggars she'd seen. She sketched a scene of a man with a downturned mouth sitting on the sidewalk. People passed by without noticing him.

I told her that it was nice of her to give the man in the wheelchair money, but that he hadn't wanted to beg. It enabled him to hang on to a shred of dignity if he could sell something. Lilia nodded thoughtfully.

"I want to come back in the future and help the poor," she said. As her mother I frequently worried that she would end up like that guy in the wheelchair selling homemade ashtrays, that she would have to live in a group home and sort screws for a menial wage. I was moved by her ambition.

That evening, we ate our dinner of lentil salad, tossed greens, cheese, and bread bought from the supermarket next to our apartment hotel. Outside, the Eiffel Tower glittered, like thousands of gold coins thrown against the night sky.

Suzanne Kamata is the author of five novels, including Indigo Girl, *and the editor of the anthologies* Call Me Okaasan: Adventures in Multicultural Mothering *and* Love You to Pieces: Creative Writers on Raising a Child with Special Needs. *She received a grant from the Sustainable Arts Foundation in support of her mother-daughter travel memoir,* Squeaky Wheels: Travels with My Daughter by Train, Plane, Metro, Tuk-tuk and Wheelchair.

Ambassador for Autism

By Davie Silva

When people think of special needs, they usually think that the United States is the best country for support. That may be true, but I think everyone should consider options in other countries as well. From personal experience I can say that international schools can be as good or sometimes better than schools in the U.S. And, the overall experience of living in a foreign country has been better for me than just staying in my own country my whole life.

When I finished sixth grade, I had to go to boarding school because none of the schools in the city where we lived could support my special education requirements. I ended up staying at boarding school in upstate New York for two years and it was an incredible experience. This school has a farm where students take care of animals. It also has all-natural power systems, it's in the mountains, and there is so much to do on the massive campus. We could go rock climbing, hiking, cross country skiing, sledding, and canoeing, and there is even a small ski resort on campus with a homemade ski lift! The nature-based lifestyle there was perfect for me, but unfortunately it did not last very long.

There were two problems with my education there. Number

one, the school only goes up to ninth grade, and I was in eighth grade at the time. Because ninth grade is their senior year, I would have a lot more responsibilities, such as being a mentor to the younger kids, and they didn't think I would be good with that. Number two, I was falling behind academically and was being teased and bullied by some of the kids because I need help with social skills.

Because of both of these problems, my advisers and I agreed that the best option would be to go to another boarding school that could give me more support. We found a school in Connecticut for students with nonverbal learning disorders (autism spectrum disorder, Aspergers, ADD and so on) who are planning on going to college. It seemed like a perfect fit for me, and they told us things such as "We are patient and understanding" and "We know how to treat kids with special needs very well."

After less than half a year there, I realized it wasn't the right place for me after all. I felt that the staff were mean to me and didn't understand me or my needs at all. They did things like not letting me take high-level classes because they said I wouldn't be able to succeed. None of the other students were interested in the outdoors; they only wanted to be on their computers all day. The school staff made me feel bad about myself; that there was something wrong with me that needed to be fixed. I will not give too much information about what they did because I am trying to forget about it, but they made my life miserable and I became depressed, up to the point where I refused to talk to anyone.

Luckily, I was able to escape. I did not have to go back to that same school. Instead, my dad's job allowed me to move to Uruguay with my family, and I was accepted at the American school there. I am so glad I got this opportunity because going to school in Uruguay has made my life so much happier and I no longer struggle with depression. It took a while to get used to it because, as sad as it sounds, I wasn't used to people being nice to me. Now I am doing great in school because the staff are nice to me and make me feel good about myself again. They are flexible when it comes to educational requirements and let me have necessary accommodations such as extra time on tests. I feel that they are more than happy to support me and will always be there for me — not just my friends, but the teachers as well.

I am very thankful and happy that I got to have this experience, and I really do not want to leave. Even though this school did not have a lot of experience with kids like me on the autistic spectrum, they were willing to take the time to understand me. In fact, one teacher asked me to give a speech about autism so that the rest of the community would hopefully see my perspective and that I am capable of doing great things. In other words, the staff at the school in Uruguay gave me not just one, but many chances to prove myself.

Throughout my life, I have had the opportunity to experience different ways of living. It is a very cool experience, because you can do things that you would never be able to do if you were living in only one country for your whole life. For example, when I lived in South Africa, there was so much wildlife I got to see, and it was the place to go for exclusive up-close animal encounters. I don't know any places in the United States or other countries where you can hug a chimpanzee, pet a cheetah, or feed a baby lion — all things I got to do there. I love animals, and this was a really cool and unique experience I would not get anywhere else.

Another advantage of living overseas is that you can have experiences with different cultures and try new things. I would think that if I was living in the United States for my whole life, I would get bored of certain foods and certain types of people. As an American, I love pancakes and cheeseburgers, but since I have lived in other places and have an open mind for trying new things, there are foods that I love even more. I eat just about anything from Ecuador, where my father is from and where we go often to visit my grandparents. I love the variety of seafood and amazing things they do with plantains. When comparing the taste of Ecuadorian ceviche to the taste of a hotdog, American food seems a lot more plain to me.

I've been to four different international schools and one boarding school that had a lot of foreign students. I had a Chinese roommate at boarding school, and he taught me some Mandarin words. I feel like sometimes kids from other countries are more accepting of me and my differences. Maybe it's because we are all a little different since we come from different cultures and backgrounds. So instead of thinking I'm "weird" they are just thinking it may be my culture or something from my background.

The more people are willing to give me a chance, the more opportunities I have to practice my social skills and get better at them. Here in Uruguay, I get invited to hang out with my classmates; not as much as I would like, but it's definitely better than nothing.

Whenever I live in a new country, I always end up with some cultural aspects of that country that stay with me. For instance, a common tradition in Uruguay is to have a *parilla*

— a barbecue with different types of meat, cooked slowly by the fire, while sitting outside with a few friends in the backyard on a Sunday. We do this often because we like the tradition. There are a lot of hidden things in other countries that you would only find in those countries. One of my favorite snacks of all time is *biltong* — different types of dried meat prepared with all kinds of spices. The only problem? It is only found in Africa, mainly South Africa. This means that in order to experience this delicious treat, you have to go to South Africa because they don't have it anywhere else.

One thing that is usually very hard for autistic people is to be flexible in changing environments or schools. Living in different countries means I've had to adapt to a lot of changes. This means new social interactions and new routines. I don't like it, but I can deal with it and I know that this is preparing me for life. I've had more practice meeting new people and making new friends which is helping my social skills. I've met people from all different cultures and learned that there are good and bad people all over the world.

I have a hard time at first getting used to new routines, but I can do it. For example, I really love to go fast down hills, either running or on a bike. In Serbia, there were a lot of hills and I could do this, but in Uruguay, it's all flat. I had to use my flexible brain and creativity to find other ways to stimulate this need for speed. Another example is that the doors in each house we've lived in are different, and I have to work extra hard to learn how to open them with keys. In Uruguay, our front doorknob is weird, and I slammed my finger in the door trying to close it. Now I know I have to pay more attention to my hands when I close this door and other doors. So my brain is always learning new things every time we move. I may hate this, but I know it's good for me.

So living overseas is good for me, but I also think the fact that I live overseas is good for other people, too. I'm able to show people around the world what having autism is about. I'm like an ambassador for autism, showing people that autistic people are good people; we are capable people. I gave a presentation to my high school class when I started here in Uruguay and I explained the basics about autism and also a little bit about how it works in my brain. Later, I made a presentation in our TED-Ed club about how people with autism should be more accepted, especially in high school. People may have doubts about me when they first meet me, but in the end they see that I'm a nice guy who can do the same things they can, maybe just slightly differently.

When I came to Uruguay it took a while for people to include me, because they had little background knowledge of autism spectrum disorder. To be included in groups did not take as long as I thought it would, but then there was one time when I wanted to go to the movies with a group of friends but one of them was hesitant about inviting me and unsure about how I would behave. Luckily I was able to go, and the reason why the inclusion process was quicker than I expected is because I was able to show my friends that I am a nice person and fun to be around.

There have been some schools where people have not been allowed to become a student there because of autism. Some school officials have said things like, "They will not be able to succeed in this class." This should change. More schools should give kids a chance. Schools may be worried about how they can help an autistic kid succeed, but they just need the right attitude. If they are patient and willing to try things out, they may be fine. As an autistic kid, I've had to learn how to be flexible and adapt to their world, so I think they could try and be flexible and understand my world, too. In the past two years at the school in Uruguay, I have had much luck with this.

This idea does not only apply to teachers, but to anybody I see every day at school. What I really want socially, especially being in high school, is just to fit in. Sometimes, however, it is not as easy as one may think. Therefore I really love it when people take time to understand that if I look mad it doesn't mean I am, I just have a hard time smiling when I talk to people. I make mistakes, but I learn from them just as anyone would. The friends who take the time to understand me and accept me as I am are the friends I always try to be with. This proves a point that to be around people like me you don't have to know too much about special needs, but you do have to treat special needs people nicely. Even though the U.S. may have the most experience and knowledge about special needs, foreigners who are nice and patient and willing to try and understand me have sometimes been more helpful to me than the experts in the U.S. In my experience many foreigners don't seem to judge me as much; they actually give me a chance to prove my capabilities, and they treat me with respect.

I feel I can bring awareness about autism to other countries and cultures, and I like to think of myself as an "ambassador for autism."

Davie Silva is a third-culture teenager who has already lived in six countries as the child of a diplomat. He is crazy about skiing, skateboarding, roller coasters, and composing music. He has an identical twin brother with whom he shares a secret language, and a younger sister who is jealous of that. Just don't ask him where he's from — it's too complicated.

Wonder, Miracle, Gem ... Merveille

By Cecile Dash

She is only 13 years old, or so they think. She wakes up on the concrete floor under the bed her three siblings share. The sun is rising, but in their home, it is still dark and humid. She has soiled herself once again and is covered in her own feces. Her mother wakes up, opens the door of their home, then drags her out from under the bed and moves her outside. Mother is angry once again and lets her know how angry she is while changing her clothes.

Today is a good day — the family members all go to work and school and they leave her outside. Most days, she gets locked up inside the house all day. She is thirsty and hungry, the sun is hurting her skin, and she crawls to the other side of their little plot. Their house is hidden away so nobody will see her, but they all know she is there. She eats the plants because she is so hungry; she eats everything she can find. Her feet are still bleeding from the mice that chewed her toenails last night. She tries to scratch her toes, but this makes it hurt worse as some of her toes are already very badly infected.

This is the story of Merveille.

I had given up my career back home in the Netherlands to follow my husband who was offered a great job in Congo-Brazzaville (The Republic of the Congo), but I wasn't ready to give up the degree I had put so much time and effort into prior to departing.

Africa Mercy, a floating hospital ship that docks in port cities all around Africa, arrived to Congo the same time I did, and this provided the perfect opportunity for me to finish my master's degree by doing a case study onboard this unique charitable hospital.

I made some good friends with the crew on the ship, and when I knew the ship was preparing to depart Congo, I asked if there were any local projects I could get involved in. I had finished my thesis and we were finally settled into our new lives in Africa. So, I had time to help others.

Mercy ships do much more than provide free surgeries; they train locals and do screenings to identify people with other medical needs. Herma, the wife of the Mercy ship's hospital director, found Merveille while screening the local neighborhoods.

I decided to join Herma on a trip to visit Merveille. We went down the muddy path in a nearby neighborhood to her home. It was humid and hot, with mosquitos flying everywhere. We arrived at a wooden shed at the bottom of a very steep hill. Inside was a fragile, extremely dirty little girl who seemed to be six or seven years old. The smile she gave when she saw us went straight to my heart. This was the day I first met Merveille, and she would unknowingly change me and my perspective of the world forever.

Merveille was born a healthy girl, and although the family faced severe poverty, they were happy. Another daughter came along after Merveille. When Merveille was three years old she fell ill, but the family didn't have the means to pay for medical treatment or even for her to visit a doctor. Like most Congolese in similar situations, the family prayed for her to get better. She didn't, and the effects of her illness (meningitis) left her severely handicapped.

In Congo, the stigma attached to having a handicap is harsh; people thought she was possessed by the devil, and the family became outcasts. Soon after, the father left the family, and Merveille's mother was in a dire situation. After years of struggling, she remarried and had two more children with her new husband. Her new husband never fully accepted Merveille and treated her like a "thing" rather than a human being. He didn't want to feed her or care for her at all.

As Merveille grew older the effects of her disease became more apparent. She didn't develop the way her sister did, she didn't grow like other children her age, and she never learned how to speak. She couldn't walk and had little control over her tensed-up muscles. Her legs didn't bend, and she wasn't toilet-trained. Always being put in the same seated positions led to bedsores in those areas, and her hair had a reddish/orange color due to severe malnourishment.

The community tolerated Merveille and her family, but they didn't integrate much with them. They pitied and feared them. This sounds horrible, but the circumstances that this family lived in and the lack of education can provide some explanation. From my judging (although I am not a doctor), her mother suffered from depression, but in a country this poor, that is a luxury disease.

I continued to visit Merveille weekly, to wash her, feed her, play with her and sing to her. Communication with her family was difficult due to the language barrier and the fact that they always needed something from me — money, medicine, food, school fees for their other children, etc.

I wanted to change and improve her situation but failed to come up with a sustainable solution and lay awake many nights contemplating this. So I did what I could. I brought back suitcases full of large diapers whenever I traveled abroad. I sent video footage of her to handicapped clinics in my country and physiotherapists, and they in return gave me tips and tricks of how I could improve her situation.

However, I found the advice they gave me wasn't working in her situation. For example, they told me to bring playdough or other toys to stimulate her hand coordination, but her family needed money, so they would sell whatever I brought. They were in survival mode, and I had to try to respect and understand their situation.

Meanwhile, Merveille spent every day either locked up in their wooden shed or left on the side of the road half-naked. She was extremely malnourished, and diapers were only used on the days I visited because they sold the rest for extra money. The progress was slow, and most times it was as if we took one step forward and seven steps backward. I felt defeated.

Luckily, I found someone to help. Mamam Rebecca, a Congolese widow who worked with me in a local orphanage and lived near Merveille's home, had recently retired and was struggling to survive since there were no such thing as pension funds available to her. I decided to hire her to take care of Merveille so she would have an income again. Her job was to visit Merveille on a daily basis. She cooked meals and fed her, washed and massaged her. Like me, she became very attached to Merveille.

Merveille's situation stabilized for the time being. However, I knew I would leave Congo in the near future, and I felt there was more I could or should do.

Tensions between Mamam Rebecca, Merveille's family and me were high and the novelty of my visits was wearing off. They wanted cash from me, and every week I visited there was another issue or problem. The family blocked Mamam Rebecca from visiting Merveille and started to spread rumors amongst the other villagers. The whole situation spiraled out of control. Finally, we decided to seek help from the village chief.

In Congolese culture, every neighborhood (quartier) has its own chief who is the most respected man in the community, and his word is the law. In most cases the chief is also the richest person in the quartier, living in the largest house and driving the most expensive car. Nonetheless, the chief seemed impressed that we approached him for help and gladly offered to intervene.

We met in Mamam Rebecca's house — the chief, Mamam Rebecca, Merveille's mother, Ernest (my driver and translator), others from the village, and me. We had to wait for the chief; for the Congolese, that is a sign of power; the longer you wait for someone, the more important they are. I could tell by how everyone behaved around him that I needed to show him respect, which made me even more nervous. With the language barrier and the cultural barrier in which women did not normally speak up the way I did, I could only hope my message would come across positively.

As it turned out, the chief and I got along quite well, and after a few very uncomfortable conversations between Merveille's mother, Mamam Rebecca and me, the verdict was in our favor. The chief agreed with us about Merveille's urgent need for better care. We were given permission to continue caring for her, but as a result, Merveille's mother felt resentful. The chief's word is law, so she had to obey, but she made sure we knew she wasn't happy about it. If we wanted to care for her so badly "then you can do it all" was her attitude.

We decided to take Merveille to Mamam Rebecca's house more often; she could sit in the village courtyard and have some interaction with the children nearby. Mamam Rebecca would carry Merveille on her back from her house up the hill in the hot Congo climate. In the meantime, we could see the changes in Merveille; she was able to eat and drink independently and was more gentle with others.

Nevertheless, I continued to have more sleepless nights worrying about Merveille. I had spent four years visiting her. How do we continue? Ideas swarmed my head: Should I adopt her and take her with us when we leave Congo? Should I start a handicapped school in Congo? It doesn't make me feel better just visiting her; it only rubs the unfairness of her world and mine in my face. I would fall asleep thinking about it all and finally decided on trying one last time to search for facilities or clinics that could help her.

A friend offered to help, and we started our search. We found two schools for handicapped children and were told by both principals that they only accept children with autism. We could clearly see that half of the students at the schools had Down syndrome but no, according to the principals, they were all autistic. How do you begin to improve conditions for people with special needs in a country where most of the population is desperately poor, education is lacking, and there is no place for the handicapped? When sick or disabled, you pray or you turn to black magic. There aren't many other options.

Our last stop was a polio clinic, where we were again told they couldn't help someone like Merveille. The gentleman speaking to us saw how defeated I felt, and as I walked away, he ran after me and suggested that I speak to Madame Potignon. He explained that she had a handicapped daughter and owned a few clinics as well as a school for handicapped children in the area.

This gentleman played a huge role in the changes that happened in Merveille's life from this point on. I contacted Madame Potignon, and the next day she demanded to see Merveille in one of her clinics. The interaction of this 70-year-old woman with Merveille was magical to watch. Where Mamam Rebecca and I were afraid of hurting Merveille when we touched her, Madame Potignon knew just how to handle her. Within 30 minutes, Merveille was setting one foot in front of the other with support from Madam Potignon. Merveille was visibly comfortable with her, and the entire time at the clinic she was smiling. She wasn't as tensed-up as she would normally be and even made shrieks/ laughing sounds.

A few days later, Madame (now Mamam) Potignon took us back to the polio clinic that turned us away the first time and much to my surprise, this time they said Merveille could get treated there. Because of our connection with Mamam Potignon, we received the VIP treatment. They started her on muscle relaxers and taped her legs to correct their position every other day, along with physiotherapy and massages. All of a sudden there was improvement; we were now seeing Merveille as a young woman, not just a handicapped child. It was incredibly emotional for me to watch her drinking and eating by herself, pointing to things she wanted and beginning to use some of the flashcards I had made for her to communicate.

The first time I brought along the flashcards, I was confronted with a big cultural difference. My flashcards were of a toilet, a shower, a glass of water, a plate of food, etc. — Western pictures that I printed from simple google searches. What I quickly realized is that their toilet is a hole in the ground, their shower is a tin plate structure with a bucket of water inside, and their glass of water is a plastic handle cup that the whole family shares. So I threw my cards away, took pictures of everything at their house instead and started all over. This time we included facial expression flashcards too, with Mamam Rebecca as a model.

Merveille began spending most days and nights at Mamam Rebecca's house. Her sisters would come and see her every day, and her parents appeared pleased with how Merveille was doing. Although I wished they were more involved, they seemed more relieved that she wasn't living with them anymore. Things were finally stable, and Merveille was making progress.

My last hurdle was to maintain the care she was receiving, as it brought along many medical costs including Mamam Rebecca's salary as well as food, clothing and diapers. Mamam Rebecca basically adopted Merveille as she was spending all her time with her, caring for her like a daughter. I knew that my family would be leaving Congo, but I felt I owed it to Merveille to find a sustainable solution.

Merveille was put in Mamam Rebecca's custody with consent from her family. Mwana Villages, the orphanage I was working with, took Mamam Rebecca and Merveille under its wing of protection financially and medically. I arranged for a local expat community to get involved. With the expat community, we set up an NGO that will continue supporting Merveille and Mwana Villages.

My heart is filled with joy, and at the same time it hurts knowing that there are many more children locked away in wooden sheds across the country with no hope or future. This is where I think of a friend of mine I met in Congo who told me; "One child at a time Cecile, focus on that, one child at a time."

My family relocated to Dubai. We are adjusting to a new life coming from such an extremely impoverished Congo to the other end of the spectrum in Dubai. I am still involved with Mwana Villages and get regular updates on Merveille's progress. I never thought in a million years I would get this attached to a country and some of the people in it, but it hurts my heart to be away from them. Life in Dubai makes it even more difficult. It's hard to adjust to the amount of wealth and excess all day long when I know that so many people could really use some of that wealth in Congo.

I went back to Congo for a visit. Merveille and Mamam Rebecca had moved from Pointe Noire, a coastal city, to Nkayi, a more remote village inland. Mamam Rebecca is in charge of a new center opened by Mwana Villages. As if it were meant to be, I found Merveille the perfect wheelchair along the way. Being reunited was the best feeling in the world. Merveille must have gained at least five kilos and looked very healthy; her hair was braided nicely and back to its normal color. Her hands and feet were healed, and there were no more bedsores. She gave me the biggest smile and held my hand; I know she was happy to see me. I spent a few nights with them, and the progress she made was truly remarkable. She can crawl out of bed, and if you tell her to get into the shower, she will move herself toward the shower. Even when I was washing her, she moved around to make this easier on me. This time as I was leaving Congo, I was on an emotional high. I finally felt like I had helped Merveille as best I could.

Update: On the 28th of May 2019, Micheline Potignon Ngondo, or Mamam Potignon as I knew her, passed away unexpectedly at the age of 74. She was a widely known and respected woman who advocated for vulnerable children and women in Congo. She introduced a child protection bill — the first of its kind in Congo — that was later adopted as the Potignon Law in 2010. She went on to ensure passage of another bill for the rights and protection of widowed persons in Congo. Maman Potignon was also my friend. She helped Merveille and me when we needed it most, and she showed us love, kindness and generosity. She once wrote to me, "You have to love them in order to protect them." I am dedicating my story to Mamam Potignon as a token of my thanks for all she has done.

Cecile Dash is a passionate mom of three, volunteer, and humanitarian with a masters in "problem-solving." She put aside her professional career when an opportunity presented itself for her family to move to the Republic of Congo. She began keeping a journal from the first day, and some of her stories were previously published in the anthologies: Once Upon an Expat, Life on the Move *and* Knocked Up Abroad Again. *Cecile continues to advocate for the vulnerable in Congo through Mwana Villages.*

Remote Therapy Has Changed the Way We Think of Face-to-Face Interactions

By Erin Long

There is nothing else in the world like our ability to communicate. To this day, I remember the moment in a college child development class when I realized I wanted my career to involve helping children communicate. After graduate school and a satisfying job working with kids, however, my husband and I decided to take a chance on something different.

When my husband joined the U.S. Foreign Service, it seemed like the most exciting thing that could happen to us. Yet there was a constant fretting in my mind that I would never be able to work as a speech language pathologist (SLP) while living abroad. I thought I might take some time off and figure it all out, then reinvent myself and still have a satisfying career — but that wasn't what I truly wanted. Becoming an SLP had been a long and rewarding road. I kept rolling it around in my head: how could I use my skills while living abroad to help individuals with communication disorders? The answer came faster than I could have ever imagined. Within the first week of our first posting outside of the U.S., in northern Mexico, I had a client. That wasn't just luck; I soon realized there was a need out there that was not being met.

Word spread quickly that there was an SLP in town. The schools were glad to hear about me, and my phone began ringing. I quickly adjusted my thinking and decided I didn't need to take a year off to figure out what being in the Foreign Service community meant. I was going to continue being an SLP and follow my calling to help children. To this day, I am thankful for the first family who asked me to see their child in their home. That was not a place I had ever envisioned working as a therapist, but it was perfect for the child. Next I found myself sitting in an open-air church working with the child of a missionary family. When you are working without an office, you become very flexible about using available space.

It was phenomenal to start working so quickly, but I never dreamed that families in different countries were also finding out about me. By chance, someone in the U.S. had been researching overseas posts and came across my husband's self-introduction, in which he mentioned I was an SLP. The family contacted him and decided to take an assignment in Mexico so their child could get therapy with me. It was astonishing to hear that people were scouring every bit of information about posts around the world to find a speech therapist for their child.

What I learned during our first assignment abroad in northern Mexico was that although good health care was easy to find, and English speakers were common, special education in general had not been developed as a full discipline. Both locals and expats confirmed this. More importantly, however, it appeared that worldwide, expats were looking for learning support and specialists to help their children.

Our second move, to Brazil, was similar to our experience in Mexico. Right away, people were happy to hear that a speech therapist had come to town. This time, the American school had a learning support teacher, and the school allowed us to work together. The two of us determined the best strategies for helping children with learning differences. The best part of this experience was that once again I didn't have a dedicated office — my clients and I were often out under the endless blue Brasilia skies working together. Again, my husband and I found that good medical care was available, but special education and rehabilitative services were not widely accessible. There were Brazilian speech pathologists, but English was a problem: If you could find a specialist for your child, you still had to worry about the language barrier. There were also some ethical concerns — it was unclear whether the focus of some practices was the client or the money they wanted to charge expats. All this pointed to a worldwide need that was bigger than I had ever imagined.

By the end of our tour in Brazil, it hit me hard that I was once again saying goodbye to kids who still needed help. My work was not done, and I hated the feeling that there was nothing more I could do. I had seen more than a few families in Mexico and Brazil who were struggling to get their kids the services they needed. That was when the learning specialist at the American school asked me if I had ever heard about online speech therapy. I knew immediately I had to figure that out and make it work.

Of course it wasn't easy; online therapy was completely new to me, and I could not envision exactly how it would work or what it would look like. Luckily we were heading back to the U.S., and I spent months learning everything I could about "telepractice," or online speech therapy as most people call it. At that time the American Speech Language and Hearing Association (ASHA) was pouring a significant amount of time and research into telepractice. ASHA recognized the shortage of SLPs in the U.S. and wanted to develop online therapy as a way to reach underserved populations.

Suddenly, life as a speech therapist became even more exciting and challenging. I talked to everyone doing online therapy and went to every training available. It was a buzzing new crowd to become a part of. We had an agreed-upon goal: We had to get this right and start meeting the needs of underserved populations and individuals, not only in the U.S. but around the world. None of us had become SLPs to only do half the job.

It's now 2019, more than 13 years after my husband and I rolled into Mexico, and I know I've provided the opportunity for more individuals to access speech therapy than I had ever imagined. People from familiar locations like Australia to the most remote, like Mauritius, have reached out to me to ask about services for their children. My practice quickly became a company, because I alone could not meet the needs of all the families that were contacting me. Of course, once the company become widely known for providing speech therapy, people began to ask, "Can you get me this or that for my child?" Soon I found myself adding occupational therapists and reading specialists to my team to meet our clients' needs. My time spent working with the telepractice community allowed me to hire therapists who had established the gold standards for online therapy. They have helped train the occupational therapists and education specialists who work for my company.

The road to establishing online therapy as a valid delivery model was rough at first. Many clients came to me hoping online therapy was a better alternative to nothing, but they expected little more than something akin to Skyping with faraway family members. Technology, however, was on our side, and parents were thrilled to see the quality of the online sessions. We see and hear each other in real time, and online platforms allow the therapists to interact with the children in a very natural manner. We can draw together, play turn-taking games and truly get to know one another.

One of the most unexpected benefits of online therapy has been the presence of parents during the sessions. Parents become part of the therapeutic process and are able to continue the work we address in the actual session. Considering that almost any therapist will spend less than one percent of a child's week with them, parent involvement plays a critical role in accelerating the benefits of therapy.

What I could never have guessed is that online relationships could be as meaningful as face-to-face ones. We start off in much the same way as with in-person introductions — the polite "getting to know you" phase — but most relationships with clients blossom into true fondness for each other. When the opportunity arises, I meet up with clients in person. I am always amazed by the genuine closeness we feel as we greet each other with hugs and kisses. Online therapy has brought us together, as we face challenging situations and overcome them through effective teamwork.

Almost nine years after beginning to offer online therapy, it might seem that I would know exactly how it works and what to expect for every client, but that's not quite how this story ends. Of course, I no longer wonder whether online therapy is a good idea. Online speech therapy, occupational therapy, tutoring, and psychological counseling have all become widely accepted, mainstream modalities for delivering services. The benefits have been endless. Today, children with rare illnesses and disorders can have access to the best specialists available.

My company supervises graduate students from George Washington University who are doing their externships. It is now expected that new speech pathologists should be knowledgeable about providing online services. As time passes, more and more medical and educational specialists are realizing that at some point in their career, they will be working with remote clients. Online therapy fits naturally into the mobile lifestyle of Foreign Service members or anyone moving around on a regular basis.

Yet within the expat community, families face unique challenges in cities around the world as they seek to identify and secure special needs services for their children. The education plan for each child is different. Many of our clients receive one service that they get after school. Some clients, however, need a bit more, and that is when our skills and creativity are put to the test. Some kids are just too tired after school, so we work with the schools to find a time during the school day to hold sessions.

For cases requiring multiple intervention services, we take a team approach with the school to determine how we can best serve the child. Often we draw up an Individualized

Education Program (IEP) equivalent that stipulates what the child needs and how those needs will be met. For example, a child may receive reading lessons online with a reading specialist while his classroom teacher teaches literacy to the rest of the class. The child is given extra time for assignments and tests. To make sure he or she does not miss too much time with peers, speech therapy sessions are held at home after school.

There are many different ways online services can meet the needs of the child with a learning difference. Perhaps most importantly, however, I have come to realize that all therapists and specialists must understand the challenges families face with moving so often. It is usual for a child to regress a bit after a long summer break, but when a big move to a new country is added, we must recognize that the whole family is going through a time of both excitement and grief. It is my mission to help kids and their families as they move around and to listen for what they really need as they establish a new life in a new home and school.

Families going abroad with a child with special needs should ask themselves: What are the most important considerations for us as a family and for the child that needs help? I am continually impressed by the open-minded approach most families take. They survey the landscape, become advocates for their children, and put together a plan that takes into account their child's unique needs. This often involves a great amount of trial and error, but it is always with the most sincere aim: to help their child thrive.

It has been my great privilege to work with so many of these families. They have opened their homes and hearts to me and become an important part of my life. We have worked together when their child was struggling and celebrated together when their child succeeded. I'd like to thank all of them for allowing me to be part of their journey.

Erin Long is a speech pathologist and the owner of Worldwide Speech. As a global nomad herself, she understands families in transition and how mobility affects them. She has developed an extensive understanding of the educational challenges children face in the international school setting, and her goal is to make special education services available to families everywhere. Erin enjoys bouncing around the world, putting down roots wherever she, her husband, two children and one little dog go.

An Atypical Childhood: Raising an Autistic Child in Japan and Macau

By Kevin M. Maher

I didn't realize Atticus was so difficult until Norma was born. I didn't realize Japan was challenging for autistics until I moved to Macau. I didn't realize any of it, but I certainly remember it.

At two years old, Atticus hadn't been diagnosed as autistic yet, but in reflection it was obvious. We couldn't take him anywhere. Our apartment was child-proof, and all things were locked up or placed at the highest point in the room. Anything within his reach would be manhandled, ripped apart, broken, or destroyed. Plates, dishes, and cups were equally on lockdown. Any food item that was left on a table would soon be all over the floor along with the broken dish. For him to drink anything, we had to hold cups to his lips since we knew that he loved to see how liquids spilled, particularly over his head. We thought that was the norm for raising little ones.

Atticus developed a habit of howling like a wolf, but with off-key pitches and repetitive tones, the same syllables being uttered over and over again. We would ride trains in Japan, where any loud person having an animated conversation received particularly disapproving looks. Atticus would get the look, but it would be replaced by forgiveness for being such a cute little *gaijin* (foreigner) baby.

He also developed into "Atticus the Launcher," as I called him. He'd launch his milk bottles from his baby carriage towards the most inappropriate places. People all over Japan would pick up "the accidentally dropped" bottle with a huge smile on their face while looking at the cute foreign baby. "*Kawaii!*" Yeah, he might have been cute, but our backs were sore from picking up the things he launched. He would outgrow it, we assumed. Isn't that what all little kids probably do?

We put Atticus in day care, not because we were both working, but because we hoped it would help him develop language. We were exhausted from the "Does he speak Japanese?" questions, particularly since we knew he couldn't speak or understand English either. We were continuously reassured that the delay was normal because his mind was processing in two languages.

The day care experience didn't last long for him. We were blamed for not being able to control him. He was intolerable. He ripped up books as opposed to reading them and was always escaping the classroom to play with water in the bathrooms or to push elevator buttons. These *gaijin* kids without any constraints, just doing whatever they wanted to do!

In the summer, we had a holiday from the university where I

taught in Japan. We decided to take Atticus to Michigan, to try to find a specialist for him. We suspected something on the autism spectrum, but we hadn't ruled out deafness. He never responded to any command, not even to the sound of his own name. If he couldn't hear us, how would we teach him anything? But hearing clinics weren't able to give us the answer. The test included, "If you hear a sound in your right ear, raise your right hand; if you hear the sound in your left ear, raise your left hand." Since these hearing tests were based on verbal communication, there was already a flaw in the system.

Equally, the U.S. system of testing for autism had other faults. U.S. health insurance overused the label of autism. A specialist in the suburbs of Detroit charged us $2,000 to spend 30 minutes filling out a basic questionnaire about Atticus. "Does he/she respond to his name?" Check box No. "Does he/she mimic things he hears on TV?" Check box No. One meant he was autistic, one meant he wasn't, but more were in the spectrum than out of it. Our "validation" consisted of a form letter that described a typical autistic child. It wasn't a diagnostic test at all; it was a $2,000 letter to give to insurance companies so that other experts could look at him and charge even more for their services. That being said, other autism specialists did legitimately confirm that he was on the autistic spectrum.

By the end of the summer, we were back in Japan. We still weren't able to help Atticus communicate, but at least we weren't spending a fortune on experts. Within the Japanese health care system, we were able to do an MRI scan of Atticus' brain, for a fraction of the price of the American "box-checking" diagnostic test. The MRI proved that Atticus could hear since it was registering within his brain. The problem was how he processed those verbal sounds.

We continued seeing more experts, and the Japanese themselves, like specialists in the U.S., also had a mix of opinions. Some said he was certainly on the spectrum, while one psychologist was convinced that we just need to "talk" to him. He spent ten private sessions crawling around on the floor with Atticus, asking him questions in English. "Oh, you like trains? Why do you like trains?" We just needed to ask him more questions, he insisted. Eventually Atticus would respond, and it would unlock a torrent of vocabulary that was sure to astound us. He was simply a late bloomer, the doctor reiterated. Being the desperate parents we were, we questioned why he assumed we weren't already doing that, but we followed through with the sessions anyway.

Still, most Japanese people assumed he was normal and perceived his oddities as just an undisciplined *gaijin* foreigner kid. They overlooked his lack of interaction with the verbal world as something from the Japanese/English translation divide.

As for us, it was obvious that he didn't care for the verbal world, but he was engrossed in the visual world. He was obsessed with watching things fall or be thrown. He adored dropping things off of the kitchen table, with their loud landing thuds, or their spiraling movements downward before their ultimate impact. It was as if the objects moved in slow-motion in his brain, and he was registering them at every angle. Equally, the way that water moved was a mesmerizing and exciting sight. He appeared to be recording it in his mind, exciting himself with his flicking fingers and flapping arms, completely drawn into the experience. The pleasure he gained from that seemed tenfold to what a wine

194

enthusiast might experience on a once-in-a-lifetime visit to French vineyards. Atticus was able to feel that excitement any time he watched something fall.

Like many other young boys with autism, he became enthralled with Thomas the Tank Engine. He cried when his YouTube clips were turned off, and he knew the location of every Thomas the Tank Engine toy in any store within our city.

The shop with the largest selection was one kilometer downhill from our house, through a labyrinth of narrow and winding back alleys that were easy to get lost in. Atticus and I would navigate those alleys, me leading, with seemingly different outcomes every time. Because of the occasional car or downhill coasting bicyclists, I would hold on to his hand tightly. But in the rare moments I would let go of him, he knew where to go. It shouldn't have been too surprising to me that at three years old, he had mentally memorized the exact maze-like path from our apartment to that store.

While at work one day, my wife called me to say that Atticus had run off around a building, and then promptly disappeared. Immediately we created a search party, and by calling and texting everyone we knew, we went on a campus and neighborhood hunt for Atticus, which involved both the campus and city police. Two hours later, we received a call from a police officer that Atticus was sitting at the police station with a handful of Thomas the Tank Engine items. Apparently, he was picked up at the cash register of his favorite store, believing that once the trains were given to a clerk, they would be his. Store employees called the police and they picked him up. I imagined that he wouldn't let go of his coveted Thomas toys without a serious fight, and they let him keep them. When I went to the station, I was expecting him to be crying or distressed, assuming any three-year-old would feel that way after being lost for several hours. Instead, he was blissfully jumping around the station, laughing to himself, like it was his best adventure yet.

Meanwhile, Atticus' visual strengths continued to shine through, particularly with puzzles. Once he became familiar with any puzzle, he would reach and grab a handful of pieces with one hand; individual pieces sticking out every which way between his clenched fingers. One by one, he removed a piece from his hand and placed it in a spot he felt it should be. At first it looked like isolated puzzle pieces randomly placed, but as he continued, all of the images started filling in. My colleagues and friends were so impressed that one of the university professors insisted on filming him.

All in all, Japan's tolerance of Atticus was decent. However, the services available to foreigners were inadequate. They simply didn't have the services available in English, and no school or day care was equipped to accept him. Atticus didn't adhere to any Japanese social norms, nor was he expected to do so. It was stressful knowing the social rules and being unable to teach my child to conform to Japan's expectations of behavior. The howling on trains, the inappropriate throwing of items, the demands to play in fountains or with faucets of water: all were becoming too much. The questions remained for most Japanese, "Why would they allow him to do these things in public?"

It's not that Japan didn't have people with autism. Once I had Atticus, I recognized them everywhere. A young 18-year-old student would wander about the campus, and had the typical flapping arms and pacing back and forth when stressed. There was also a severely autistic child I would see with his father in a public city swimming pool. The young teen flapped and splashed simultaneously, laughing his head off, with his serious-faced father leading him down the swimming lane. They were well-accepted — tolerated — at least from what I could tell.

But Japanese culture is known to keep thoughts within, so it was not possible to know what a Japanese person really thought. Would they readily categorize my son as an autistic, or did I have too many unknowns? Was he just a little *gaijin* of a foreign family with limited Japanese abilities who couldn't adhere to Japanese social norms? Or was I just being a self-conscious father, eagerly trying not to be the square peg in a society that preferred round ones?

Regardless of that, my world changed again when Atticus was four and my second child was born. My daughter was completely respectful, attentive, interactive, and made us feel like the greatest parents in the world. I bonded with her immediately, and I didn't have to spend time teaching her things like "Don't pour water over your head," as I did with Atticus. She allowed me to discover what other parents felt like on a regular basis — she was a child who connected with her parents. She idealized, loved, and wanted to please us.

People with neurotypical children (non-autistics) aren't aware that meaningful interaction is rarely experienced with autistic kids. My daughter showed me that I could make a kid smile, laugh, and learn. Her existence also taught me to see the child-behavior of my son and not solely the autistic behavior.

After Norma was born, we moved to Macau, an Asian city

with a history of foreigners making a long-term home within its borders. We found schools and autism services in English. What wasn't available in Macau, we easily found in Hong Kong, a one-hour ferry ride away.

While there are a large number of services available to Chinese-speaking parents in Macau, it's rare to find an Asian city that accounts for foreigners with special needs services in English. Fortunately for all of us, an English-speaking Venezuelan woman had previously broken autism ground before us as a long-time advocate for her own teenage autistic son who was born and raised in Macau.

Additionally, the region allows locals and foreigners alike to legally hire a domestic helper. Atticus has an assistant who works with him at school and at home, which has proven to be invaluable to us. This was also something we could never afford if we had gone back to the United States.

Emotionally, as stressed parents, we found an indifferent Chinese population that seemed to lack rigid social norms, unlike Japan. The Chinese tended to be louder and less interested in their surroundings. In Japan, a launch of a toy would be met with a gasp. In Macau, the thud of it would be drowned out by a significant amount of other noises happening simultaneously. There were rarely reactions to Atticus' unusual behaviors.

It's been eight years that I am an American raising a foreign autistic kid in Asia. Half of Atticus' life was in Japan, and the other half in Macau. Japan was difficult, but we've now found a supportive school, a full-time helper, city resources and services freely available, and plenty of community, tolerance and support in Macau.

These days, Atticus struggles but attempts to use basic communicative English when required. He is nowhere near the linguistic level of his sister, but she invites him into our language-oriented world. For years I struggled with a gnawing in my heart that I would have to leave the expat life to raise an autistic kid. It hasn't turned out to be the case.

We've only traveled part of the journey, but things have been coming together. We have a team now: my wife and I, our domestic helper, my daughter, Atticus' teachers, his school, and the services provided in English by the city of Macau. We are helping him along on his own journey.

Through it all, there have been many voices — some stressful, some self-reflective, and many of them helpful. My autistic son has remained voiceless. But, if I observe the voicelessness enough, I hear the messages. Atticus might be non-verbal, but non-verbally, he consistently speaks the "Just let me be a kid" message the loudest. I will put more effort into listening to that one.

Kevin M. Maher is an American who has been teaching English abroad since 1996. He has had short stories published in the United States, South Korea, Macau, and Hong Kong. You can find a full-length book of his entitled No Couches in Korea *on Amazon.com. He continues to live in Macau with his wife and kids.*

Let Me Hug Her: Elisa's Story

By Nayeli

Note: This story was compiled from a series of text messages and voice recordings in Spanish sent to our editors by Nayeli, an undocumented Mexican immigrant in the United States. We have tried to preserve her unique voice and her spirit in this English-language version, and her last name is withheld for her protection.

I am writing this while I'm sitting in front of my daughter Elisa on the floor in her intensive therapy session, seeing her there so tense, and not being able to do much of anything. I talked to the doctor, and although I have complete trust in this hospital specifically, it doesn't stop me from hurting when I see that there isn't much they can do at this moment to help her feel comfortable, only to hope that her lungs recover and they can give her medicine without compromising her life or her health. Because if they give her medicine now, it can make her lungs stop working or her blood pressure drop too low. So I have decided to start writing after spending two days trying to soothe her, and thus this is the way I am starting to share our story.

We are from Guadalajara, in the state of Jalisco, Mexico. I

arrived in the United States two years and one month ago. I have spent the last seven months in Colorado, and I've been living in a shelter for victims of domestic violence.

My daughter was born in Mexico in 2013 with Down syndrome. She was a very healthy little girl, and within the parameters of her condition she was an exemplary child. Not just because I say so — she really was; even at the University of Guadalajara they used her as an example of what a baby with Down syndrome can achieve when provided with plenty of love and attention. That's how my baby was.

But … when she was only one year and eight months old, she became sick. She had a high fever, and very early in the morning, we took her to the hospital. Even wrapped up in blankets, she was shivering with cold. We spent about 16 hours in the emergency room begging for her to be treated.

Unfortunately, when she finally received treatment, the nurse mistakenly injected her with Neomelubrina (dipyrone), a drug that is banned in more than 30 countries, including the United States. This nurse was behaving so negligently and so arrogantly towards me and my daughter that I don't think she even realized the serious error she had committed.

This medical error caused embolisms in Elisa's heart and her brain. I saw how my little girl started to struggle to breathe. I shouted out for help, and I saw that my daughter was turning dark blue. She looked like a fish that had been taken out of a tank and was gasping for air. Her gaze was fixed on me the whole time … but I couldn't do anything to save her life, except call for help. All of the nearby staff ran toward my daughter, they surrounded her, and thus began our ordeal, in

October 2014, in Saltillo, Coahuila, Mexico.

After two long months in intensive therapy, they finally released her. No longer a healthy, thriving girl with Down syndrome, she now had severe brain damage, due to a human error which could have been avoided. My daughter will never walk or speak again. She has cortical vision impairment. She has epilepsy. She can't eat by herself. She can't even suck on a bottle to drink.

Now I can look back and see how both Elisa and I developed resilience. Now, the days are not all bad days. But it hurts to remember.

August 9, 2017

I've just been in the hospital with Elisa in Colorado, and we don't really know what is wrong with her, but thank God, everything is a little calmer now.

I'm living in the Gateway Shelter; it's not for children with special needs, it's for victims of domestic violence, but they help you find resources. They recommended I apply to the Coalition for the Homeless to get a three-room apartment, and they would support me for two years without asking for payment. If Elisa, God willing, needs more time to recover, they will even extend the time.

It has been a long and very difficult process. I have been in Colorado for eight months, six of which I have spent living in a shelter, but with great, great patience, with God and with love, things are working out.

September 2, 2017

The insurance in Colorado doesn't pay for all the therapies and medical equipment. I have to go to the hospital and pay $15 for each treatment and each piece of equipment. So I try to get the needed equipment from donations.

Going directly to emergency rooms has often been a good strategy for me, since the people there help direct me to specialists my daughter needs. First I was in Los Angeles, later in Houston, and now I am in Colorado. In my experience all of the states are different in their treatment of immigrants and of children with special needs. In the case of Colorado, one of the programs I was able to access was the "Charity Program," which is limited and a bit difficult to access, but it helps the child continue treatment in the United States. Another is called the "Butterfly Program," which I recently joined. It is for families with children who are very ill with chronic and perhaps terminal illnesses. They guide you, hold your hand, help you preserve memories, and help you come to terms with the idea that your child may have a high risk of passing away.

Another important strategy for me has been listening to my social workers and staying in close touch with them. They provide help to me both as a mother and a migrant, making sure the children have full support, and offering to help me access the type of programs I need.

I've encountered both support and prejudice from people in the United States. Mostly, people see me in this situation and they want to help. As a mother, I know that they have their own lives and they can't always help. A child with special needs requires a lot of attention. In my case, I can't work, and if I sleep four hours it's a lot. People do support me. They give me a ride, or they say, "Here, I'll pay for your bus ticket." Many people are very open. I think it's a matter of the attitude you take in life. There are people with prejudices, but I choose to take a positive attitude toward the circumstances. I know clearly that in Mexico I would be in a worse situation, since there we don't have the same type of accommodations, such as buses with ramps, donations, and connections to medical specialists. Here, there are Facebook pages for parents of kids with special needs and their relatives, and for those with children who have died. There is no shortage of people who can help, but I've found it's always important to remember to be active, to stay in contact with my social workers, look for resources — on Facebook, among friends — and be open.

I've been reflecting on the situation of families with special needs in Mexico and in the U.S. As Mexicans, we are very family-oriented, and in contrast it seems to me that the U.S. has a very materialistic culture, but living with special needs can be less complicated in the United States. In the U.S. it is very easy to access services that make life easier, which may not exist in Mexico because of its more limited economy.

But it's also a question of values, it comes from the parents. Whether special-needs children are seen as deficient or are appreciated and admired, that comes from the parents and from education. There is discrimination both in Mexico and the U.S., but the way you view your own children affects the way others will see them. I have seen situations in the U.S. when a special-needs child is seen as a problem and a burden, and some parents say, "You know what, I can't do it," and they take the child to a special place to be taken care of. From before birth, the doctor may say "Your child has a problem, there are options," but in my case I said, "She's my daughter, I love her." Both in Mexico and the U.S. I've seen cases where parents fully accept these children, or where they sink into frustration and annoyance, or where they say, "I can't" and give them up for adoption.

I'd like my country to do more in education and values. There is a lack of information about children with special needs, and what families can do. Often a disability can be prevented, for instance a mother may be an alcoholic or smoking during pregnancy, or a doctor may harm the baby by mistake. We can raise awareness about all of these things. Also, I believe that no one can take care of a child with special needs better than the parents, but the parents need to know what to do. Doctors and nurses can make mistakes and cause disabilities, as happened with my daughter who can't walk and can't see because an overtired nurse gave her the wrong medicine. I haven't confronted this nurse, but I know that in the U.S. they give more time for medical personnel to rest, as well as more recognition, and medical teams have what they need. The infrastructure in Mexico is lacking, and if we could fix this, there would be fewer children with disabilities. Of course there are also genetic accidents, but everyone should be more conscious about the risks.

In the United States, I've learned that to get help, I need to open myself without hesitation, without shame, and doors will open for me. It's hard, it's tiring, but I need to appreciate what I have. In Mexico, the laws call for special schools, but they are poorly equipped, without the resources to truly help special-needs families. I think that's why I emigrated. In the U.S. there is more. The Telethon exists in Mexico to help kids with disabilities, but my daughter has a chronic illness and they wouldn't accept a child in her situation. Every therapy is expensive, and the public health system is terrible in my experience; that's why I decided to move to the U.S.

Now I sleep very little. Elisa was not born in the U.S., so we get less support, but there is even less in Mexico, that's why we're here. But I don't have a nurse who can help me take care of her. I'm so tired and sometimes my body just can't anymore. I take lots of vitamins, try to take naps, and try to take rest days when I don't go anywhere. Other days I have to take my daughter along with me and do what needs to be done. I listen to happy music and work hard to create a cheerful environment; I keep everything neat and clean, and I surround myself with positive people. This is what helps me face my situation.

With her sweet face typical of Down syndrome, my daughter looks a bit like a little Japanese girl, but she is Mexican and now we are in the U.S. I think that's funny. And speaking Spanish and learning English brings many humorous moments. I joke with the nurses, and that makes staying in the hospital a little more agreeable. They call her "Ee-LY-za" instead of "E-LEES-a," which makes me smile, and they always admire the way she's dressed up. Another thing I think is a little bit funny is that every time we are getting ready to go out, just at that moment she soils her diaper, but these things happen.

When I go out with Elisa in the wheelchair stroller, some people criticize; they don't know she has special needs. Actually, my whole situation is pretty ridiculous and even comical when I think about it: me without papers, sometimes out on the street. We never know what life will bring us.

My little girl is chubby, she can't talk, but she opens her eyes and gives a little laugh, "huh-huh," it's so cute. My days and moments with her are so special. In the shelter, I live with other women from different cultures: Africa, South America. They all view the situation with my daughter differently, but we all manage to see life with joy. I think that's what a child with special needs gives you: valuing life, enjoying the little things. When someone is going through a hard time herself, and she sees me, she says "wow," and she doesn't see me with pity but with admiration, which is beautiful. It's something I enjoy about being here. Because it is so painful to have a child who was damaged by a human error, but at least I can help others a little bit with my example. It makes me feel that yes, it is terrible that this happened to us, but we are all here to help each other. And in the end what happened to my daughter wasn't in vain. I'm so sorry about the cross she has to bear — for myself I don't see it as a burden — we have had many good moments.

I can't dwell on negative things. Yes, it's been hard, but you learn to value things. I think this is what has led me to view life as I do now. It's so sad that we have had to look for help from the government or a lawyer to get the support my daughter needs. But always, the way of looking at life is most important, as well as the people around us — there is never a lack of people who are willing to extend a hand. Not always the same person, but someone is always there.

I've learned a lot, starting from being humble. Humility is very important, because you never know what life will bring you, no? And I think the greatness of human beings is found in humility.

What is incredible with Elisa is that she can't move, she can't communicate, but she has touched the hearts of many people. In fact, I laugh about this: a cousin told me, actually not only one cousin but many people have told me, "Let me hug her! Let me touch her!" and they feel that they are getting a positive vibration from my daughter. And yes, really, I think people like her were sent by God because He wants us to value our lives through them. I say, was this really necessary? But one has to see the positive side. And one more thing I have learned from my daughter is to love life, no matter what the situation you're in. To see her big, beautiful eyes, it's so glorious, and to value every little moment, every little movement she makes, and I think this has made me grow as a person and I notice that I appreciate what I have. I think every parent of a special-needs child will be able to say this, and it's something I try to share when I can: love life. There's always someone in a worse situation than you, sadly, and instead of demotivating, it motivates you, you say, "I can do it," and that's that.

September 19, 2017

My baby passed away on September 11. And I have to tell you, for sure she is an angel. I'm right now in the apartment we were waiting for since I left her dad. The Coalition for the Homeless just gave me the keys for my apartment which will be paid for two years so I can get up on my own feet again. I applied for this back in March, and I was looking for the perfect place to live with Lisita (Elisa) since August. The day I signed for her funeral these people called saying that they had our apartment approved to move in right away. They didn't know that Lisita had just passed away ... they were surprised and so sad, but Lisita has left me with a lot of resources in place for me to continue my life.

This sounds like a lot of coincidences for people who don't

believe in angels, I know. During eight months I was waiting and fighting to give her a better life ... and in a week, the week she died, I feel like everything came from God. EVERYTHING.

I am in debt to Heaven, to God, but mainly to my daughter. I am so glad to be able to tell her story here. It is the least I can do, and I have to do it thanks to what my daughter left to me. I wanted to share the blessings and miracles she gave me.

Nayeli was born in Guadalajara, Jalisco, Mexico, After studying music at the University of Guadalajara, she worked for three years as a flight attendant for Volaris, a Mexican airline. She currently works at a Korean restaurant and is in the process of receiving her U.S. residency permit. She now lives in an apartment of her own, thanks to help from the Coalition for the Homeless, with her 2-year-old daughter Nicole, whom she describes as "very independent and noble." She still misses Elisa every day, but she says that seeing her story in print has helped reminded her what she is capable of. Once she has her residency and can travel internationally, she wants to give talks in Mexico about avoiding errors due to overconfidence, a topic about which she also learned a great deal during her time as a flight attendant.

Bridging a Cleft

By Elisabeth Weingraber-Pircher

We looked at each other trying to understand. What had just happened to our baby, our life and our future?

My husband, Gerd, and I were sitting in a small windowless room at Cambridge University Hospital. We had been ushered here straight away following the three-month ultrasound of my second pregnancy when the technician detected a cleft lip. Now we were waiting for the cleft surgeon and a specialized nurse. After a while I said, "I remember making fun of a friend in elementary school for his funny pronunciation, but we loved him the same." Gerd nodded, adding, "It can be repaired, right?" Then silence fell again between us until the nurse came in.

She immediately rattled off information about treatment options, possible health-related issues and recommended tests. During her monolog, she repeated several times that a cleft was no reason for abortion, a shocking statement for us as this thought had not crossed our minds. We knew we would love our baby with or without a cleft. So why mention abortion? Were a cleft lip and palate worse than we had thought? Even the meeting with the surgeon to discuss interventions during the baby's first year left us insecure.

During the drive home we gazed at the English countryside gliding by. We were both far from our respective birthplaces and families in Austria and Italy. We had been married for seven years, with a two-year-old keeping us busy. Cambridge was our seventh home on our third continent together. During those transitions we thought we had learned to deal with uncertainty and surprises. This, however, was suddenly more intense and personal. It was about our baby and our life. How were we going to handle this?

We longed for more information and did extensive internet searches on cleft lip and palate care in the U.S., Austria, Germany, Italy and of course the U.K., only to realize that more data was not helping us at this stage. Information was not the answer to our fundamental question: How will we deal with our son's birth defect? We sat down with our favorite thinking aid — a glass of red wine — and started a conversation about our feelings and hopes for baby Gregor's life.

Slowly, a clearer vision emerged. We were ready to embrace this challenge and deal with it as best we could. We promised each other not to make his condition the center of our or others' attention. Instead, we wholeheartedly decided that Gregor should be defined by who he is as a whole person, and by how much he is loved. We vowed not to treat him any differently than his older brother.

In practicality, this translated into seeking advice only from professionals without indulging self-titled "experts" on the internet, as well as telling people about the cleft at the same time we mentioned other characteristics about our future child. In the future, it would mean answering questions our child would have about his cleft lip and palate only to the point he was interested. We turned this big issue into a small part of our everyday lives. But even with a clear vision from a philosophical point of view, we still needed to work out the more concrete steps on how we could support Gregor over the next few years.

As many expats know, a move comes when you least expect it. My husband is a permanent expat for an international bank, and we move based on business needs. These can change rather quickly. A few weeks after our fateful visit, my husband called me with his usual intro, "Honey, will you still love me if we move to ..."

Of course, this move was to happen one month before Gregor was due. Without a fixed address in London, our new home, I could not register with a General Practitioner, which meant I was obliged to go to the emergency room at the nearest hospital to give birth. The rigidity of bureaucratic process without any inclination to acknowledge the exceptional circumstance and the inability to plan for Gregor's birth left me very frustrated. In the end, friends saved us. They connected us with a private gynecologist who referred us to a good public hospital and cleft center.

Just a few days after moving house and four days after meeting our new neighbors for the first time, we knocked on their door asking them to watch Thomas the Tank Engine with our toddler while my husband rushed me to the hospital. My water had broken earlier than expected and Gregor was born one hour after we made it to the hospital.

For the first time I felt lucky that Gregor was considered a "complex case." In the UK, all cleft cases get pooled by region and assigned to one experienced cleft consultant. Once we decided to trust him and his team of cleft nurses, speech therapists, orthodontists, and psychologists, we felt at peace and did not feel the need to look for alternative methods. This proved to be a wise decision and gave us time to bond as a family of four.·

Since cleft babies cannot create suction to breastfeed, several feeding techniques have been championed by different clinics. Our cleft team advised us to use soft plastic bottles and squirt the expressed breast milk into the baby's little mouth. Gregor embraced this technique because he swallowed well and was always hungry (and continues to be 14 years later). My day consisted of expressing, freezing and heating milk, disinfecting bottles and feeding the baby, with a 90-minute break before restarting the cycle.

On top of this, we wanted our toddler, Leopold, to have a normal busy London toddler life, and so I took him to gym, art and music classes with Gregor in tow. I was constantly exhausted, as was my husband, who fed Gregor every night despite having to catch flights at 6 a.m. or lead important meetings the next day. I remember looking at my husband feeding Gregor in our bed at three in the morning while I was expressing milk and thinking that this was not exactly how I had envisioned our life as parents. But it was moments like that that brought us closer; we were in this together.

Another excellent source of support was the specialized cleft nurse who came to our home. She checked Gregor's growth and advised on cleaning his palate and nasal cavities to avoid infections. And, she helped with the violent reflux Gregor had developed, which sometimes caused him to stop breathing. Besides the reflux medication, the nurse was armed with tried and tested solutions for any new issues we faced. We greatly appreciated her help, especially after we realized these home visits are not standard practice in other countries.

After 18 short months, during which we managed to find a comfortable routine for Gregor's unique situation, we were told it was time to move again. This time we headed to Düsseldorf, Germany, where we discovered that the cleft center at the hospital near our new home used very different techniques and timelines for lip and palate repairs. In the U.K., Gregor had undergone the following procedures: a cleft lip closure at four months of age and a palate closure (without the use of a metal plate) at nine months. However, when we moved to Germany, we were confronted with a different timeline and a German cleft surgeon who strongly disagreed with the timelines initiated by the UK team. He favored using a palate plate despite the fact that it required frequent adjustments due to the rapid growth of a baby's face, and a palate closure procedure at a later point.

Since we felt strongly that Gregor needed to have a local, open-minded doctor in each new city to identify potential problems early on, we looked elsewhere, even if that meant spending multiple hours commuting to a new practice with two and later three children. During our time in Germany, Gregor not only underwent ear tube surgery to alleviate his constant ear infections (a common side effect of a cleft), but he also started speech therapy in our native, home language of German. Around the time a child loses baby teeth, an alveolar bone graft is necessary, taking bone from the hips and transplanting it into the remaining opening of the palate. Again, timing varies from six to 12 years depending on the centre. Following the timeline of our U.K. consultants,

Gregor had the bone graft procedure back in the U.K. when he was 11 years old.

Despite our many postings, which have brought Gregor from Cambridge to London (U.K.), to Düsseldorf (Germany), Milan (Italy), Woking (U.K.), São Paulo (Brazil) and back to Milan again, where we are currently based, we continue to privately see our original cleft team in the U.K., once a year, for an annual checkup.

The South Thames Cleft Centre is the one place outside of our home where all of Gregor's medical records are collected and where people have known him since birth or shortly thereafter. This continuity of care allows us to see progress or lack thereof and identify potential issues. We found that sometimes local doctors applied only their national standards to Gregor when they examined him. For example, his Italian pediatrician considered Gregor overweight, when in fact he continued, with his usual growth spurts, perfectly along the same weight percentile since birth, as documented back in the U.K. Similarly, a local dentist recommended braces because two teeth were growing on his palate, whereas his regular dentist asked us to wait because one tooth had moved forward unaided previously. Prior to Gregor's arrival, we had already applied this principle to other medical specialists, like our pediatrician and dentist in Graz, Austria, where we spend our holidays and do our annual checkups.

These medical visits not only ground us in our wandering lifestyle but they also keep the cultural variable stable. Culture is defined as the learned and shared worldviews of a group of interacting people and greatly impacts how we, as members of a particular culture, view illness and health, particular conditions, and the status of medical practitioners. One of the central functions of culture is to define how we deal with birth, death, sickness and health. Do you pay a doctor to cure you or to keep you healthy? In our case, we noticed cultural differences in each of the places we lived.

For example, in the U.K., cleft cases are covered by a multidisciplinary team, assigned depending on a patient's postcode with limited possibility to change teams, similar to the state school system. In Germany, we had a choice between competing centers who were sometimes dismissive of each other, which made us feel rather insecure. Moreover, in the U.K., the underlying treatment philosophy was minimal intervention and achieved mostly via home care by visiting nurses. The emphasis was on getting mothers to use breast milk for feeding, but not to actually breastfeed. Germany's underlying focus seemed to be constant observation and adjustment of palate plates to allow for breastfeeding. The importance of the act of breastfeeding seemed to outweigh the constant trips to the doctor and the metal object in the baby's mouth.

A diagnosed cleft lip and palate in Germany allows patients to access the handicapped person's support system and apply for benefits one feels entitled to, whereas in the U.K. the support of the assigned team is deemed sufficient. In Brazil, I observed in the private health care system that Brazilian physicians tend to be more involved and take more initiative. For example, when Gregor needed to have a tooth surgically removed, the local dentist not only coordinated with our team in London to find the most suitable specialist in São Paulo, but she was also present in the operating room to hold Gregor's hand, since parents were not allowed inside.

The good relationships we developed with the local doctors were priceless, especially when we were assigned to the U.K. and Italy again. How fabulous it was to arrive in a country and feel like we were visiting old friends when finding familiar faces in our old doctor's office. How wonderful it was to see my son ease into an orthodontist's chair in Milan and hear the doctor joke with the consultant about how Gregor had looked as a child. It takes time and effort to build such trusting relationships, yet it is worth it in the long run.

And speaking about worth: The fact that Gregor does not consider his repaired cleft lip and palate a defining feature of his life has made five operations, countless visits to different medical professionals, yearly flights to London and two folders filled with translated medical reports worthwhile. The fact that he does not mind medical visits as long as no needle is involved is a credit to the doctors. In a life that consists of constant change, to have Gregor's core cleft team stay the same was important to him and to us. It also allowed us to use them as a sounding board as we made decisions or searched for doctors elsewhere. Another aspect of traveling to his annual checkup, that has become an extra bonus, is the substantial one-on-one time Gregor enjoys with one parent. In a family of five, that is precious.

Another insight that has gotten us through the years was to not get stressed by the "advice" we received from well-meaning family members and fellow expats. We decided to pick the most suitable aspects from each medical system and culture we've lived in and blend them to what works for us.

Over the years we have tried to translate our vision of focusing on love and normalcy by treating hospital visits like any other everyday errand: clothes shopping or driving to

Taekwondo competitions, for instance. When people looked at Gregor and were seemingly itching to say something, we would say, "Yes, the young man has a cleft lip" without indulging further.

During Gregor's fourth grade year at school, when the visibility of his scar became an issue, we started to point out others with cleft conditions who are successful in areas that Gregor is passionate about, like science, mountaineering, and acting, to show him that having a cleft is by no means a restrictive aspect. On the contrary, Gregor now feels that meeting others with the same condition is like finding instant friends. Books on cleft lip and palate issues were as available as books on science and animals in our house. Only once did he come home from school saying that someone had made a derogatory comment about his scar. After an explanatory email to his teacher, she dealt with it in class effectively. That year, Gregor and his best friends decided to fundraise for a cleft NGO; the following year it was tigers in India again.

As an expat child he has to endure curious questions every time we move during the first weeks at a new school. So we discussed what his "ready-made answer" could be, but he hardly ever needed it. Certainly a question on his cleft is slightly less irritating than a comment about kangaroos, or people singing songs from *The Sound of Music*, when Gregor explains that he is Austrian.

Thinking back to our first conversation in that windowless room in Cambridge, we now know, "Yes, the palate and the lip can be repaired" and "Yes, our child is loved all the same, if not more." It was and is a journey for Gregor and for us as his parents. As he grows older, Gregor is becoming more involved in the decisions surrounding his health and his cleft. Someday it will be all his, just like the decision if he as a cross-cultural kid will want to settle down somewhere or continue to move around.

Elisabeth "Elle" Weingraber-Pircher is an intercultural trainer and executive coach with a passion for engaging difference to achieve excellent outcomes in complex environments. What better way to expand her range of practical cultural examples than living and working in over 11 countries on four continents, being married to a loving Italian, raising three TCK boys (a never-ending story), running after a dog and seeking happiness on horseback? She is always curious about the next place, and only held back by her dislike for packing and unpacking boxes.

Mari's Story: Can you Continue in the Foreign Service after a Child's Life-Changing Diagnosis?

By Francesca Kelly and Mari O'Connor

Mari O'Connor holds up her smartphone and records her son Christopher singing "Happy Birthday" to his father, who is traveling. She prompts "Happy," and Christopher sings "Birthday." Giving a shy smile, he walks, holds a toy, and sings the entire song on key. It's remarkable that he can do these things simultaneously.

Christopher, born in 1992, is 27 years old. He has an extra partial 15th chromosome, also called "Dup15q syndrome," or "IDIC 15." There are various genetic conditions and syndromes involving the 15th chromosome, and most are quite rare. They can manifest in a variety of symptoms, including autism, developmental delays, inability to form words or even speak, seizures, and poor or missing motor skills. Christopher has every one of these conditions.

Mari and her husband Chris were near the end of their first

Foreign Service posting, in Chile, when Christopher was born. Already the parents of two daughters, they realized that something was wrong when their son was just a few months old. After two serious cases of pneumonia, Christopher was authorized a medical evacuation (medevac) to the States. Mari and the three children decided to go to her parents' home in Minnesota while Chris finished out the last three months of his tour in Santiago. They were slated to start their next tour to Colombia very soon. But first, they needed answers.

At Minnesota's Mayo Clinic, doctors tested Christopher for cystic fibrosis due to the recurrent bouts of pneumonia and failure to thrive. When that hunch proved incorrect, they reassured Mari that the baby's health would most likely improve now that he was out of Santiago's heavily polluted air. Meanwhile, Chris returned to D.C. for training in preparation for their next posting. Mari and the children joined him in temporary housing in Arlington, Virginia, where a pediatrician advised them to take the still sickly Christopher to an allergist at Johns Hopkins. Says Mari, "At that appointment, I mentioned that Christopher had been doing an odd movement for the past month: a jack-knife of his body, like Superman, snapping in half at the waist."

This description set off alarm bells with the allergist, who immediately called a prominent pediatric neurologist, also at Johns Hopkins. He was able to see them the next day. By that time Mari had made a video of Christopher's strange movements, which she showed to the doctor. The specialist was blunt. "This is an emergency," he told Mari and Chris. "Your child has infantile spasms. He needs to be hospitalized immediately."

"Chris asked, 'Are you telling us that our son will die?'" recalls Mari. "The specialist replied, 'He likely won't die, but you may wish that he would. His brain is being destroyed by these seizures, and he could soon be in a vegetative state.'" Mari and Chris were in shock.

Christopher spent the next week in the hospital as his seizures were brought under control. The initial diagnosis was Lennox-Gastaut Syndrome (LGS), which means lifelong seizures and almost certain brain damage. And yet, it appeared that the usual hypsarrhythmia that accompanies infantile spasm disorders — in which brain wave activity is recorded on an electroencephalogram as chaotic and abnormal — was not present, clouding the diagnosis.

Christopher was sent home from Johns Hopkins on two anti-seizure medicines. The family's upcoming assignment to Bogota was cancelled. Says Mari, "Chris's career development officer bent over backwards, finding Chris a job in the Political Military section at the State Department." At this point, someone gently suggested that Chris convert to Civil Service. "But that wasn't our dream."

Still, they found more permanent housing in northern Virginia, and while trying to determine their next steps, they were, almost overnight, flooded with their household effects, coming from Chile and from storage. Mari was suddenly facing an almost overwhelming future. "I had boxes everywhere, three little kids, and I was so depressed," she remembers. Then, just when she needed her most, Mari's mom, Marilyn, arrived on the doorstep. "That pulled me out of the worst of that depression. My mom was taking things out of boxes and asking, 'Where should I put this?' and I was forced to deal with it all. In the end, her visit was a huge help."

Boxes aside, the family was still centered on Christopher's medical issues, searching for the right "cocktail" of anti-seizure medications that would inhibit seizures while also allowing normal development. Here, the story takes an interesting turn, as Mari relates.

He was still very, very ill, [with] constant ear infections ... so we had him seen by an ENT at D.C. Children's Hospital, and he recommended putting tubes in his ears, but first wanted to have genetic testing done since Christopher had 'soft' signs. The soft signs included two hospitalizations for pneumonia, epilepsy, developmental delays, low muscle tone, very high palate, slightly low-set ears, epicanthic fold of the eyes, and the bones in his hands and feet are a tad irregular. This doctor was writing a book on how frequently ENTs are the first to recognize genetic issues in patients. He took multiple pictures of Christopher's eyes, ears, inside of his mouth, feet and hands. In some medical books, Christopher's pictures are featured as "Patient C."

The genetic testing led them to a "wonderful" pediatric neurologist, who found the answer at long last: Isodicentric Chromosome 15 Syndrome (IDIC15), a rare chromosomal abnormality that wreaks havoc on normal human development. "The neurologist asked us, 'Do you want to know his future?' We nodded, and she went on, 'He will need 24/7 care for his entire life. He will probably be severely to profoundly disabled, autistic, and he will likely suffer from lifelong seizures.'" Mari adds, "All of these predictions were spot-on."

In light of this new diagnosis, Mari and Chris asked the

neurologist at Johns Hopkins — who had diagnosed the seizure disorder — why he hadn't ordered genetic testing. Mari was shocked by his response: "What difference would it have made? Now that you have learned that he has a genetic issue, you will have limitations on his abilities. That's why I didn't order genetic testing. The information doesn't help." Mari replied, "Now that we know it's genetic, not the polluted Chilean environment, not something that happened during the birth process, not something that can be fixed, we can help him." Knowing they would be in the Washington area for the foreseeable future, they decided to work with the neurologist at Children's Hospital who had given them the correct diagnosis.

Although this diagnosis was dire, it was also, strangely, "freedom, in a way," says Mari. The family could now formulate a plan. "Some in the State Department were urging us to consider staying in Washington, changing to Civil Service, but that's not the life we wanted. We decided that, as long as we could get the proper medical care for Christopher, we would continue living the overseas life we had envisioned. What doctors told us was that while he was not educable, he was trainable." With that in mind, the family began the hard work of continuing with a Foreign Service lifestyle under very different conditions from which they had started.

Nearly all Foreign Service spouses learn quickly that many unexpected and unpaid tasks fall in their laps over the course of their husbands' or wives' careers. But Mari's responsibilities were monumental. While in Washington, she started researching accommodations for Christopher, starting with the State Department, sifting through its many regulations and allowances. She later decided to set up supervisory care for Christopher through a neurologist at Mayo Clinic, near their home-leave address; between his doctors there and the Department of State Medical Services (State/MED), Mari could get a list of neurologists and other resources in various overseas cities.

That was only the beginning. Each potential overseas assignment demanded hours, days, even weeks of research, to discover what specialists were available, how quickly the family could fly back to the States if necessary, which medications were available locally and which they'd need to ship to post; the state of emergency services; the cost of care; if school programs for special-needs and developmentally disabled children existed, and in what language; what private teachers might be available, etc. All of this was combined with parenting three young children, one of whom would require toddler-level care the rest of his life. While the worst of her depression lifted with her mother's help in those first few months, a more chronic depression settled in for the next two years. (Mari lost 40 pounds, which she refers to as the "silver lining" of that time.) Despite these difficulties, the family forged on, even though, at this point, there was no guarantee that a Foreign Service life was even possible.

This was largely due to the fact that Christopher was not cleared by the State Department Medical Office ("State Med") to be posted outside the United States. But his dad Chris had spotted a reasonable posting: Ottawa, Canada. Could they possibly make this happen after all? They spoke to their Mayo Clinic neurologist and discovered he had a colleague in Ottawa. Says Mari, "We contacted that Canadian neurologist, who agreed to accept our son as a patient." Mayo Clinic Neurology would continue to take the lead on prescribing Christopher's care. "This was our first attempt at doing this, and it worked brilliantly since the Mayo Clinic neurologist and Ottawa General Hospital neurologist had worked together," Mari explains. "We also contacted the Ontario Ministry of Health and they agreed that Christopher could become a patient of their children's special-needs program. This is a similar program to the one that he had participated in while we were living in Arlington. It involved an infant developmental program, followed by a specialized preschool, occupational therapy, physical therapy, speech therapies and developmental support."

With a neurologist and developmental program in place in Ottawa, the State Department cleared Christopher for this posting, and they were able to attempt their first overseas assignment following his diagnosis.

The four years in Ottawa were a success with regard to educational and medical support for Christopher. Mari now knew what she had to do to get an overseas assignment approved — and with each successive post, it became easier. Ottawa was followed by The Hague, Lisbon and Dublin. The two English-speaking foreign countries — Canada and Ireland — made it relatively easy to find special-needs schools, programs and caregivers whom Christopher could understand. In Portugal and the Netherlands, Christopher needed a translator while at school.

Simply stating that the family "made a Foreign Service career work with a special-needs child" ignores the many compromises each family member made. For Chris, career opportunities were limited by Christopher's medical clearance. For Mari, life was consumed with Christopher's care, balanced with raising the two girls. For Christopher's sisters, family life was and always would be centered around

Christopher, and both learned to help care for him as they grew older.

When the State Department initiated a new policy after 2003, sending many more Foreign Service Officers to dangerous postings where family members could not accompany them, Chris, a former Marine officer, was called upon to take these assignments, while Mari handled family life without a partner. For example, the family extended their assignment to stay a fourth year in Dublin while Chris went on alone to Iraq. Although this was hard on the family, Dublin also offered excellent support for Christopher, and the stress of moving again was postponed a year.

Mari claims that a few things helped them continue as a Foreign Service family with a severely disabled child. One was pure luck: Christopher's seizures — the biggest threat to his well-being — largely subsided between the ages of six and 18. Another plus was that the State Department was flexible about homeschooling and generous when it came to allowances for hiring private teachers.

And, connecting with other families who were dealing with syndromes caused by 15th chromosome abnormalities was enormously helpful. "The way I found the best help," says Mari, "was through finding others with the same diagnosis. It was rarely diagnosed back then: there were only 52 known cases in the world when we received our son's diagnosis. Now it's closer to 1,400 — but many more remain undiagnosed." Finding emotional and practical support from others in the same boat has become much easier in the past decade through the use of the internet and social media.

And, Mari is grateful to the embassy community members

the family encountered throughout their career. "They were always super-supportive. Always kind, probably because they knew I was kind of 'stuck' at home with Christopher, carrying a heavy burden."

The family's assignments were limited to countries with First World amenities. "We were almost posted to Sarajevo, but a State Department nurse nixed that, saying, 'There is no way we can support this kid in Sarajevo.'" Mari admits that was probably the right decision.

As the family grew older, dynamics changed and changed again. His sisters, always devoted to him, still needed to leave home for university. Despite Christopher's mental capacity of a two-year-old, his body became that of a man. He was prone to the same emotional and physical changes, such as mood swings, as any other teenager going through puberty. Finally, Chris retired from the Foreign Service and the family eventually set up residence in Minnesota, where they are now.

The daily routine, though, has not changed much over the years. According to Mari, it goes something like this:

We wake Christopher by 7 a.m. (to ensure that he has his morning anti-seizure medicines before the levels of those drugs become dangerously low in his bloodstream), shower and dress him, feed him breakfast, snack, lunch, snack with mid-day anti-seizure medicines, dinner, snack with evening anti-seizure medicines, trying to keep his medication levels, energy and weight up. Our days are spent keeping Christopher safe, healthy and entertained. Walking since age four, he needs to move to remain healthy, but cannot walk for too long, so he uses a wheelchair for distances.

Christopher has also been able to make some unexpected strides over the years. To their delight, his family members discovered that Christopher responded enthusiastically to music, and that ushered in an era, continuing to this day, of singing with him and for him, offering him musical toys to play with, and using music as a means of communication. Each family member knows and understands Christopher intimately, says Mari.

Christopher brings great joy to us. While the work involved in keeping Christopher healthy is heavy, he is generally a happy young man. We got lucky. He frequently laughs, sings and engages happily with family, friends and people he has never met. He knows no stranger. When he hears a word that he recognizes he will sometimes break into song, entertaining all. For example, he overheard a friend talking about another friend, Lisa Gingles, and started to sing "Jingle Bells."

In addition, Christopher often uses music — songs in particular — as a way to communicate his desires, as Mari explains:

He still surprises us … Due to his autism he frequently presents as being seemingly oblivious to the world around him, yet he will sometimes request something simple. For example, he will "sing" (we recognize his near-words, many others don't) "Born on a mountainside" from Davy Crockett, which means he wants me to sit down and play the piano for him. Or "Puff the Magic Dragon," meaning get my guitar out and entertain him, now, or "Bouncy bouncy," meaning "Let's go jump on my trampoline in the backyard!"

Christopher keeps my husband and me moving. While our retirement years are significantly different than we had imagined, we have our own "special purpose" to be healthy and involved in life, a reason to wake up every morning at six, a reason to keep fit to take Christopher out on the ski slopes in a sit-ski so that we can hear him yell, "Wheeee!," laughing his head off in happiness. And, who knew, but by having Christopher we have not yet experienced being empty nesters! Yes, we miss our two grown daughters terribly, but it's been a bit easier for us since we remain active in one of our children's lives.

My husband and I are now experts at taking turns, going off on small adventures with friends, leaving the other competent parent in charge of Christopher. Living overseas, my husband was the wage-earner, gone on several temporary assignments to Iraq, while I was home, running the household. In retirement my husband has embraced learning how to be a full-time, hands-on, parent. This enables us to have the freedom to enjoy adventures with friends. For Chris, off to Chicago to stay with a friend, going to museums and eating out. For me, Hawaii in March, staying with my brother, traveling with a sister and two friends, while my husband stays home, caring for our son. Is this everyone's dream of perfection? No, but it works for us.

One of Mari's great strengths has been knowing how to research possible overseas assignments so that every conceivable need of Christopher's will be addressed. Another is her ability to be honest with herself and others — sometimes brutally so. Since Christopher's seizure episodes have increased steadily since the age of 18, Mari acknowledges that Christopher may die before his parents.

The scientific research and evidence on 15th chromosome disorders demonstrate that epileptic seizures are often a cause of death. Mari and Chris have prepared themselves for this possibility. And, Mari says that in one way it might actually be a blessing: He would avoid going into a state-run group home upon the death of his parents, which would be very different from the life he has now at home. Although she can't imagine life without him, Mari adds, "I don't want to imagine *his* life without *us*."

That said, Mari has done the research and necessary paperwork that will ensure Christopher's care should they predecease him. "Growing ever older, which I'm thankful for, has been humbling but causes me to worry about Christopher's future. Every year we lose some of Christopher's fellow IDIC 15 'sisters and brothers,' and I think, at least those parents no longer have to worry about their child's tomorrows."

Mari has spent years studying not only Christopher's condition but also adult allowances and benefits. Mari urges other parents of special-needs children with profound disabilities — children who will require the same daily care when they are adults — to begin research now. "If you have a child who is going to need support for the rest of his life, you need to start thinking about this 10-15 years out." Mari researched state and federal laws and allowances for children over 21, where support overlapped, how to get Social Security benefits, how to get social services, and which states and even which counties in those states provide the most services. Just as in researching countries and cities overseas, there is a wealth of information to be uncovered — perhaps even more so because America's state and county laws vary widely when it comes to support for the disabled. Through her research, Mari was able to pinpoint the county in her home state of Minnesota where she could get the most support for Christopher. This support includes a daily class for profoundly disabled young adults, transportation to that class, a Medicaid waiver for the developmentally disabled, and even reimbursement for diapers.

Mari's interactions with the State Department over the course of her husband's career often led to discussions on how to help special needs families living overseas. "I complained that special needs parents had to rediscover the wheel with each new posting ... and I felt that there should be a virtual support group for the parents, to help each other and share information and guidance on regulations." Encouraged by then-Education and Youth Officer Rebecca Grappo, Mari set up an email group for Foreign Service families with special needs children in 2005, called FSSpecialNeeds, as a lifeline for parents posted overseas and dealing with unique issues — issues that, often, no one else at post had experience with. The group is still active today.

Because of her extensive research into support for special needs children and her ongoing passion for sharing that knowledge, Mari won a special award in 2010: the Eleanor Dodson Tragen Award, presented by the Associates of the American Foreign Service Worldwide (AAFSW) and sponsored by the foreign affairs community organization DACOR (Diplomatic and Consular Officers, Retired). This award honors a spouse, family member, domestic partner or member of household "who has effectively advocated and promoted rights, programs, services and benefits for Foreign Service families in the tradition of AAFSW and its members, as did the late Mrs. Tragen."

Newly returned to the U.S. during her husband's final Foreign Service assignment at MacDill Air Force Base, Mari flew from Florida to Washington for the awards ceremony, not realizing that her siblings and mother had planned a surprise welcome for her at the State Department. "I walked in and there they all were," recalls Mari. "Tears just burst out of my eyes." After years of being overseas and handling responsibilities without extended family members, Mari views this homecoming celebration — and the recognition afforded by the Tragen Award — as a high point of her life.

Despite the sacrifices and outright heroism of Mari's husband, Chris, this story is not about him. And despite his struggles, setbacks and many achievements, this story is not even about Christopher. It is about Mari, Christopher's mother, who has made it her life's work — her unpaid career — to care for and nurture her son, to tirelessly find the best care and education for him, no matter where in the world they lived, and to advocate for others who also might just be starting a Foreign Service career with a child's diagnosis that has turned their lives upside-down. They can look to Mari for guidance and inspiration in their struggles not to put things right-side-up again, but to learn to cope, even thrive, throughout their topsy-turvy, nomadic adventures.

Mari Olson O'Connor, a native of Winona, Minn., holds a B.S. in music education and taught in the Department of Defense School in Keflavik. She is the wife of USMC/FSO Chris O'Connor and the mother of three grown children, one with significant special needs. She has spent her life actively volunteering with a range of "special" activities, including bringing music therapy to special needs schools (in Canada, The Netherlands, Portugal, Ireland and Florida), and supporting organizations for horseback riding for the disabled (in Canada, The Netherlands and Portugal), as well as supporting Irish guide dogs and an Irish cat rescue group. Mari currently volunteers with a Minnesota adaptive ski program and is in the process of starting a support group for parents of children with special needs.

BEFORE MOVING OVERSEAS WITH A SPECIAL NEED:

A CHECKLIST *

- ☐ Consult your/your dependent's doctors and specialists about your interest in moving

- ☐ Be clear about your/your dependent's abilities, limitations, and medical needs

- ☐ Weigh the pros and cons and decide if your family should proceed

- ☐ Reach out to other expats, including those who have special needs

- ☐ Research, research, research! (Medical services, therapies, educational resources, cultural issues, mobility restrictions, etc.)

- ☐ Find service providers who understand your lifestyle. This may need to be done after arrival, but it's nice to have something set up beforehand when possible

- ☐ Investigate telehealth if therapeutic services aren't available or don't meet your needs

- ☐ Check if your health insurance covers telehealth and/or overseas claims

☐ Re-evaluate whether your family should proceed

☐ Inform family members of the plan and address questions and concerns; make sure all family members are comfortable with the decision

☐ Learn about bringing your medications and/or having them filled locally. (Some medications cannot legally be brought in and will be confiscated.) Useful information can be found on these websites, among others:

TripPrep.com
https://tripprep.com/library/obtaining-medications-abroad/traveler-summary

International Narcotics Control Board
https://www.incb.org/incb/en/travellers/index.html

Centers for Disease Control
https://www.cdc.gov/features/travel-medicine/index.html

☐ Check with airlines about special needs accommodations if applicable; look into travel options for going home or to medical care in another country if this will be needed

☐ Reach out to someone who is already at your destination to help outline your/your dependent's needs. While not always possible, having personal support when you arrive at post is huge

☐ Scan medical documents that you will need to access and keep them in an easily-accessible file

☐ Reduce anxiety: Stick to family routines as much as possible, talk to professionals about the impending changes

☐ Maintain a healthy lifestyle and don't neglect exercise, nutritious food, and sleep

☐ Set aside for your carry-on or luggage important comfort items for you/your dependents as well as a supply of medications

*This list was started by parent coach Sharoya Ham of *Embrace Behaviour Change*, with additional contributions from our essay authors. It is not a comprehensive list, and each situation may require different considerations.

Editors and Designers

Editor **Kathi Silva** grew up in Texas with a congenital fascination for other cultures and ways of life. Soon after her twins were born, she nudged her husband into the Foreign Service so she could continue her "cross-cultural studies" while being a full-time mom. In addition to advocating for inclusion and quality of life issues for her children and others with special needs, Kathi works as a freelance editor and is completing a master's degree in education. She is proud of the small seeds of kindness and light she and her family have planted wherever they go, and she is grateful that her children have taught her how truly beautiful diversity can be. She has lived most of her adult life overseas in Ecuador, France, South Africa, Venezuela, Serbia, Uruguay and Uganda.

Editor **Patricia Linderman** is the literary editor for Tales from a Small Planet. With her husband and two sons, she has lived in Trinidad, Chile, Cuba, Germany, Ecuador and Mexico, where she worked as a writer, language teacher, translator and editor. She is co-author of *The Expert Expat: Your Guide to Successful Relocation Abroad*, and she served on the editing team for Talesmag's first book, *A Cup of Culture and a Pinch of Crisis*. She now has a new career as a personal trainer and health coach in Falls Church, Virginia (and remotely). Visit her blog at www.fierceafter45.com.

Editor **Nicole Schaefer-McDaniel** became a "third culture kid" (TCK) at the age of ten when her family moved to the United States from her native Germany. Although she moved back "home" after a few years across the pond, she eventually returned to the East Coast for college and met her future husband when she was studying in New York City, her adopted "true home." In typical TCK fashion, both of Nicole's children were born in different countries. Her family has lived in Canada, Brazil, Austria, Mongolia, and Taiwan. Nicole works as an educational consultant, writer and editor, and teaches yoga. Along with Jen Dinoia, Nicole is a Real Post Reports editor for Tales from a Small Planet.

Editor **Francesca Kelly** is one of the founders of Tales from a Small Planet. She raised four children while accompanying her husband to Milan, St. Petersburg, Moscow, Belgrade, Vienna, Ankara, Rome, Brussels and Tbilisi. Now working as a college application essay consultant, she blogs at www.essayadvantage.net. A trained classical singer, Francesca continues to sing professionally.

Editor **Jennifer Dinoia** is a Real Post Reports editor for Talesmag. Along with her husband, two daughters, and son, she has enjoyed postings in Virginia, Venezuela, Iceland, California, Nicaragua, and now Ankara, Turkey. Jen is currently the (EFM) Human Resources Assistant at the U.S. Embassy in Ankara, but has also worked overseas for the U.S. Embassy in Caracas, the International School of Iceland, and the U.S. Embassy in Managua.

Copy editor **Zoe Cabaniss Friloux**'s Foreign Service family lives in Northern Virginia after stints in New Delhi, London, Milan and Port of Spain (along with some Iraq and Afghanistan, too). She knows way too much about overseas schools and pet transport but always is looking to learn more. Her journalism degree from Brigham Young University has served her well through years of newspaper editing and now freelance work. When she has spare time, it's usually spent reading, traveling, visiting museums or debating the merits of various European soccer teams.

Since 2006, designer **Dina Bernardin** has been living and working in Africa, Eastern Europe, and the Middle East with her husband and two children. She has an MFA in painting from the National Arts University in Bucharest, Romania. She is the only American, and the only non-smoker to graduate from the program. You can see more of her paintings, collages and graphic design at dinabird.com.

Made in the USA
Middletown, DE
11 November 2019